BURY

Colin Reeve
&
Tom Fish

ACKNOWLEDGEMENTS

The history of passenger transport in Bury is complicated, ranging through the whole spectrum from stagecoaches and packet boats to light railways through horse buses and trams, steam and electric trams and steam and electric railways. Bury was only a small town but its operating area and influence spread well beyond its boundaries Both neighbouring Radcliffe and Heywood were independent boroughs with very firm ideas of their own and the resultant web of operating agreements and consequent disagreements meant that nothing was ever straightforward. For such a small undertaking there was an amazing variety of chassis and bodies within the bus fleet to make Bury an interesting subject.

A book of this nature cannot adequately be written without the help of various other people, and this was especially true when writing this history of Bury Corporation Transport. The main source was the collection of the late Tom Fish. Although born in London, Tom Fish moved to Bury where he became a bus driver with the Corporation Transport Department. This sparked off his interest in the local scene and he became well known as a local historian, creating an important collection of photographs with which he gave illustrated talks and lectures, and a copy of which is now in the care of the Bury Council Archive. Special thanks must go to Tom's widow for permission to use this important material, including the draft of a history of transport in Bury which has largely formed the basis of this book and I think it is only right that he should get credit for it.

Additionally, I must thank Stuart Garnett for his assistance and for allowing me the use of his own extensive collection of photographs. David Barrow also provided a large number of photographs from his own collection and as usual George Turnbull allowed me the run of the Greater Manchester Museum of Transport archives. The Senior Transport Archive provided even more images and finally Tony Moyes contributed some of his own pictures.

Colin Reeve
February 2013

Photo credits

ADJ	Doug Jack	MMT	Greater Manchester Museum of Transport
ADP	David Packer	RM	Roy Marshall
AM	Tony Moyes	SGC	Stuart Garnett Collection
DBC	David Barrow Collection	STA	Senior Transport Archive
CR	Colin Reeve	TFC	Tom Fish Collection
JAS	John Senior		

Contents

IN THE BEGINNING

Bury

The town of Bury stands on the River Irwell on the edge of the Pennines a little over eight miles north-east of Manchester city centre, approximately half way between Rochdale and Bolton, its name deriving from the Old English word 'Byri' meaning 'castle' or 'fortified place'. Bury dates back to the Roman occupation when a road known as Watling Street was built between Manchester and Ribchester passing to the west of the town, the line of which can still be traced in several places.

Probably the town's most famous son was Sir Robert Peel (1788-1850) who became Prime Minister of the United Kingdom and is best known as the founder of the Metropolitan Police Service.

Bury rose to prominence during the late eighteenth century as a centre of textile manufacturing and associated engineering industries, although with the decline in heavy industry it has moved towards the service sector and is now largely residential, lying as it does within easy commuting distance of Manchester. The coat of arms, granted in 1877, represents local industry at the time; the anvil for iron forging, the fleece for wool, a pair of crossed shuttles for cotton weaving and a papyrus plant for the paper trade.

Bury was first recorded as a Parish in 962 AD. It became a Borough in 1876 and a County Borough in 1889. In 1974 it became a Metropolitan Borough within the then Metropolitan County of Greater Manchester, absorbing the ring of small towns around it that had always looked to Bury for their services. It is now a Unitary Authority with a population of some 181,000 at the last census.

Stagecoaches and packet boats

The earliest mention of a regular passenger transport system in Bury is in 1796. In that year a twice-weekly horse-drawn stagecoach, which travelled between Rochdale and Manchester via Bury, was abandoned due to lack of patronage. That year also saw the start of a steam packet-boat service operated from the canal wharf at Bury Bridge. This was on 24th September when two boats owned by Messrs Craddock arrived at Bury with much rejoicing. Incorporated in 1790, the Manchester, Bolton and Bury Canal Navigation Company had been granted powers to construct a canal between Manchester and Bury with a branch to Bolton and ultimate connections with existing canals. The Manchester, Bolton and Bury Canal Company was formed on 2nd January 1791, this latter canal reaching Bury via Radcliffe and also ending at Bury Bridge. It did not go without its mishaps, however, an accident on 14th June 1818 causing the drowning of five people and a month later, on 30th July, a packet boat with a pleasure party on board sank near Withins Lane, Radcliffe.

Road passenger transport in Bury developed from the horse drawn stagecoaches that passed through the town around the beginning of the 19th century. In 1817 coaches were leaving the Eagle and Child in Silver Street for Manchester daily at 7am and to Burnley and Colne on Sundays, Mondays, Wednesdays and Fridays. By 1824 Bury was well provided with horse coaches as can be seen by this list published in that year.

'From the Grey Mare Inn, Market Place.
To Leeds and York: the Royal Mail every night at 9, through Heywood, Rochdale, Halifax and Bradford and the Neptune by the same route, every day at 12. To Liverpool, the Royal Mail every evening at 7 through Bolton, Wigan and Prescot and the Neptune everyday at 1, through Bolton, Leigh, Newton, St. Helens and Prescot. To Manchester, the Traveller every Sunday and Monday morning at 10 and on Tuesday, Wednesday, Thursday and Saturday morning at 7, returning the same evening and proceeding immediately through Haslingden, Accrington and Whalley to Clitheroe and the Commercial every Sunday and Monday at 10 in the morning and on Tuesday, Thursday and Saturday mornings at 7 and a coach every Monday evening at 7.

From The Eagle and Child, Silver Street.
To Manchester: the Comet every Tuesday and Saturday morning at 7.30, the Alexander every Tuesday, Thursday and Saturday morning at 8, a coach every Sunday,

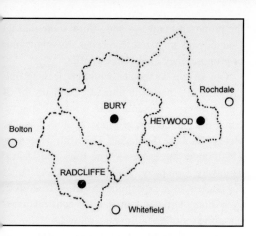

from near the Monument in the Market Place at fares of 4d inside and 3d to ride outside on top. A service to Holcombe, via Woolfold and Tottington, departed from the Waggon and Horses and the Albion Hotel three times a day. The Albion Hotel was in Haymarket Street and was demolished in 1969 for the construction of the Millgate shopping centre. The fares on this route were 6d inside and 4d outside. Other now-forgotten firms ran services twice a day from the Commercial Hotel in Princess Street to the Roebuck in Rochdale via Heywood. From the White Lion in Bolton Street, to the White Horse in Hanging Ditch, Manchester, buses run by a Will Nickson left Bury each day at 8.30am, leaving Manchester for the return journey at 11.00am and 6.00pm. Another service was run from the Grey Mare in the Market Place to Edenfield.

The Bury and Manchester Passenger Conveyance Association had a horse bus leaving the Derby Hotel in Market Street each morning for the Royal Exchange, Manchester, returning in the evening. Fares on this service, which was primarily intended for businessmen, were one shilling to travel inside and 9d to sit on the outside. In general the fares charged on these services were much higher comparatively than present-day rates, and thus this form of travel was for the wealthier people.

A frequent service of horse trams was later operated to Manchester via Whitefield by the Manchester Carriage and Tramways Company. Formed in 1880 by the amalgamation of the two major operators in the Manchester area, the Manchester Carriage Company and The Manchester Suburban Tramways Company, it ran its bright red and white cars from a depot on the corner of Bury New Road and Knoll Street, Higher Broughton. The building was still in daily use by a haulage firm until its demolition about 1989.

The railways came to Bury in 1846 when the East Lancashire Railway Company opened its Bolton Street Station for traffic to Manchester, Accrington and Bacup and the line through Knowsley Street Station to Rochdale and Bolton was opened in May 1848 by the Lancashire and Yorkshire Railway Company. Horse buses could not compete and by 1886 only the Rochdale via Heywood and the Edenfield routes were still running and in 1889 only the Edenfield service was left.

Wednesday and Friday morning at 9.30 and every Saturday morning at 7.30, a coach every Tuesday morning at 7.45 and a coach every Monday at 3 and 5.30. To Skipton, by Burnley and Colne, the John Bull, every Sunday afternoon at 2 and every Saturday afternoon at 3.30 and every Tuesday evening at 5.30 through Rawtenstall.

From The Old Boar's Head, Fleet Street.
To Colne: the Union every Sunday, Thursday and Friday afternoon at 2, every Monday evening at 7, every Tuesday evening at 6 and every Wednesday and Saturday evening at 5, through Rawtenstall and Burnley. To Manchester: the Union every Monday afternoon at 4, Tuesday and Saturday morning at 7 and Wednesday and Thursday morning at 9.

From The White Lion, Millgate.
To Manchester: the Favourite every Tuesday, Thursday and Saturday morning at 8, and the Lark every Tuesday and Saturday morning at 7.30.

Conveyance by water from the Canal Warehouse, Bury Bridge.
To Manchester and Liverpool and all parts of the Kingdom: The Old Quay Company, every Monday, Wednesday and Friday – Thomas Cooke, Agent.'

By 1838 services had been extended to Rochdale, Bacup, Blackburn and Hull. According to Heap's Bury Miscellany, dated February, 1854, a Mr Robert Lever plied horse buses to Whitefield

THE STEAM TRAMWAY

The preliminaries

In November 1869, plans were submitted by the Manchester Suburban Tramways Company for a tramway between Bury and Salford via Whitefield and Prestwich, running along Manchester Road and Silver Street and terminating in the Market Place. At that time the 'Red Flag Act' of 1865 still required a person with a red flag to walk in front of all mechanically propelled road vehicles and every new route had to be authorised by a private Act of Parliament which was a very arduous and expensive procedure. The proposal was not carried forward.

By the Tramways Act of 1870, which authorised the promotion of street tramways, local authorities were enabled to construct and own tramways but were not allowed to operate them and were obliged to lease them to private companies, although if agreed they could purchase any section in their area after 21 years.

On 26th November 1877 the Town Clerk reported that two competing companies had applied for permission to lay a tramway into the town along Manchester Road. The Council reserved its decision and again the proposal was dropped. By this time, in other towns, the preferred mode of transport was turning to steam and several plans were submitted for proposed systems within the town boundary, varying both in route and gauge of track.

In August 1880 the Council heard that the two companies were intending to seek powers in the forthcoming Parliamentary sessions to construct tramways within the Borough and, whilst admitting the desirability of building a tramway, reserved for further consideration whether it would be more advantageous to construct the tramway itself, leasing the working of the lines to a company. The Council felt that the increased facilities for travel would lead to a growth in traffic and, should the lines be well constructed and judiciously worked, that benefits would accrue to the ratepayers by their introduction.

So, on 4th September the Council passed a resolution that 'It is desirable that a scheme of tramways should be introduced' and the Town Clerk was instructed to write to the promoters of the proposed tramways and inform them that the Council was prepared to receive any application or proposal they might have to offer.

One of the companies withdrew leaving only the firm of Charles Phillips & Company of 20 Bucklersbury, London, its principal partner being the flamboyant and unscrupulous financier Henry Osborne O'Hagan. On 16th December 1880, under the name of 'The Bury and District Tramway Company' it applied to the Council for consent to approach the Board of Trade for a Provisional Order authorising the construction of a tramway system in Bury as follows:-

'From Blackford Bridge along Manchester Road and Moss Street and terminating in Haymarket Street, the line being of the 4ft 8½in gauge.'

Also the following lines on the 3ft 6in gauge:-

'A line commencing in Market Street near the Market House, proceeding along Market Street, Princess Street, King Street and Rochdale New Road and terminating opposite Pimhole Lane.

A line commencing in Market Street by a junction with the last mentioned line and passing the western side of the Market House.

A line commencing in Clough Street near the Waggon and Horses Tavern, along Clough Street, King Street and Rochdale New Road.

A line commencing in Clough Street, Stanley Street, Water Street, Moorside and Walmersley Road and terminating at Hamilton Street.

A line commencing in Market Street near the Market House, proceeding along Market Street, Old Market Place, Bolton Street, Bury Bridge, Crostons Road, Tottington Road and terminating at the Borough boundary.'

The promoters also included in their order powers to construct a line within Whitefield from Blackford Bridge along Manchester Road to the Broughton Toll Bar House.

The company contended that it would keep a large proportion of the roads of the town in repair and the line would be rated and therefore not only give the public a service but relieve the ratepayer as well. Thus a private company, without paying any royalties, would not only obtain possession of the most important streets in the Borough for 21 years, but also secure the right to be bought out at the expiry of the lease. However, having regard to the financial position of the Corporation and the probable length of time that must elapse before the

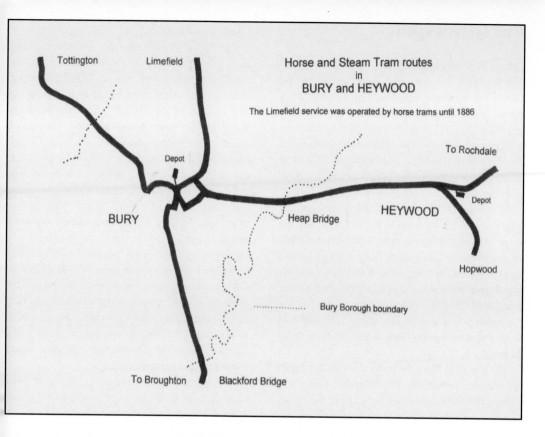

Horse and Steam Tram routes
in
BURY and HEYWOOD

The Limefield service was operated by horse trams until 1886

Tottington · Limefield · Depot · To Rochdale · Depot · BURY · Heap Bridge · HEYWOOD · Hopwood · Bury Borough boundary · To Broughton · Blackford Bridge

lines became a paying concern, the Council agreed to the proposals with the addition of the extension of the Rochdale New Road line to the Borough boundary at Heap Bridge and to the connection of the Borough, through Heywood, with Rochdale. The Order received the Royal Assent on 26th August 1881. The length of the roads within the Borough for which powers had been sought and obtained was over five miles and the lines traversed the Borough from north to south and east to west.

In 1882 the company was renamed 'The Manchester, Bury, Rochdale and Oldham Steam Tramways Company Limited' and later that year sought additional powers to extend its lines in Tottington Road to Tottington and in Walmersley Road to Limefield (Hark to Towler Inn).

By the powers obtained in the 1880 Order the tramways within the Borough were to have been completed by 31st August 1882, but up to that date only the first section of the line between Bury Market Place and Blackford Bridge was complete. This was then connected through Whitefield to a point just inside the Salford boundary at Broughton Toll Bar and was originally constructed as a single line with passing loops built to the standard gauge.

Although the Order contained strict clauses on the timescale and quality of work there were many delays causing annoyance and loss to both residents upon the line of route and to the general public who wished to travel over it. The workmanship was not to the standard that the Corporation had expected and when the lines were inspected during the week ending 10th March 1883, the Borough Engineer, Mr Cartwright, pointed out to Lieutenant General Hutchinson, the Inspector of Railways and Tramways to the Board of Trade, that in several places the line had been laid above the level of the roadway which was dangerous to other road users and the Corporation could be liable for any damage or injury that might arise. He requested that the Inspector bring this to the notice of the Company and have it see to the line before granting his certificate. Lieutenant General Hutchinson replied that as this was not a matter that concerned the safety of the running of the tramway, he could see no reason for deferring its opening! On the other hand nor could he see any reason why the Company could not comply with the reasonable requirements of the Corporation.

The system opens

Bury's first tramway opened on Monday 12th March 1883. To mark this great event in the history of the town, officials from neighbouring towns were invited and gathered at the tram depot in The Wylde. They included the Mayors, ex-Mayors and officials of the Corporations of Bury, Salford, Rochdale and Heywood as well as some Chairmen of Local Boards through whose districts tramways either were already laid or were planned. At 9am they all set off in two steam cars to travel the six miles to Kersal Bar where the inspection started. Lieutenant General Hutchinson then walked the line back to Bury to make a close inspection of the track. The Kersal Bar section was found fit for use and at 11am the first service tram used the line. This was five days after the Company's first section was opened in Rochdale from the Wellington Hotel, along Oldham Road to Buersil.

On arrival in Bury the party went on to inspect the line to Limefield. The intended route was along Fleet Street and Rock Street from the Parish Church to Clough Street (now part of Rochdale Road), then along Stanley Street, Water Street and Walmersley Road terminating outside the Hark to Towler inn. However, the Rector of Bury had obtained a protective clause forbidding steam trams to run along Fleet Street and Rock Street and in front of the church. An alternative route had originally been proposed along Haymarket Street, Agur Street and Clerk Street to Clough Street and then into Stanley Street but this was too narrow, so, instead, horse trams were used running along Market Street, Princess Street and King Street to Clough Street. This section was found to need some work carried out on it and also there were no horse cars available yet. However, by 20th March the track work had been completed and horse cars were now available so the Limefield section was opened. At the time of these openings the tram depot was nowhere near complete and only enough cars were available to give a reliable hourly service; this later being increased to a thirty minute service when steam locos and cars became available.

During the first day of operation a large number of people gathered to witness the cars leaving Bury. So many people were anxious to ride on

A vintage scene at Limefield as a horse tram leaves the 'Hark to Towler' on its way to Bury. *(TFC)*

the cars on that day, that the trams could have been filled many times over. The engines and cars worked satisfactorily and the steam trams made five round journeys covering 60 miles and being said to have carried some 700 passengers.

After the inspection, a luncheon was provided by the contractors in the Derby Hotel in the Market Place with between 60 and 70 people present, the chair being taken by Mr William Busby, the Vice-Chairman of the Steam Tramways Company.

At the time of the opening it was reported in the local paper that "The satisfactory manner in which the engines and cars proceeded over the lines of tramways must have given satisfaction to even the few who until now have been prejudiced against the use of steam. The type of engine which the Company has adopted is one which no reasonable person could object to. In appearance it is somewhat like a small tramcar. It makes no noise; neither does it emit smoke or steam. Comparatively little notice was taken of it by the large number of horses passed on the road and but a few days will be necessary to quite accustom them to its appearance."

It is worthy of note that at a meeting of the Association of Municipal Engineers held in Bury the same year, Mr Vauser, the Engineer to the Manchester, Bury, Rochdale and Oldham Steam Tramways Company, stated, *"There is every reason to believe that tramcars will, at no distant day, be propelled by electricity."* In the same week that Bury's first steam tramcars started to run, a car propelled by electricity was given a trial on the West Metropolitan Tramways Company line from Uxbridge Road to Kew Bridge in London. The electricity was stored in accumulators fitted under the seats. Even in the earliest days of Bury's steam trams there was mention of electric propulsion.

The steam tram depot was in The Wylde next to the Castle Armoury and was built of stone of a type that the Armoury front is faced with today. It covered an area of 3,600 square yards and the buildings included an engine shed which could accommodate twenty engines, a broad gauge car shed to hold fourteen cars, a narrow gauge car shed and stables for fourteen horses. These were all of single-storey and a further two-storey building comprised a repair shop, smithy, storeroom, gas engine house, coke shed, office, oil store, general

The depot in the Wylde with the Castle Armoury behind. *(TFC)*

Pictured in the Market Place is tram number 33, a narrow gauge Wilkinson type car built by the Leeds firm of Thomas Green and Sons. *(TFC)*

store rooms, workman's room and a carriage building shop. A waiting room occupied the space between the two entrances in Castle Street, the east entrance being for the narrow gauge rolling stock and the west for the broader gauge trams.

The locos were of the 0-4-0 wheel arrangement with coke fired vertical boilers built by Thomas Green & Sons of Leeds, to the patent design of William Wilkinson of Wigan. This design needed to comply with the Board of Trade regulations that steam tram engines should not emit any visible smoke or steam. Mr Wilkinson's patent comprised an exhaust superheater or steam drier that rendered the exhaust invisible. The engines were short, squat and heavy weighing about eight tons. The motion was transmitted to the rail wheels by a cog-wheel gearing. Metal side panels came down to within two or three inches of the road to cover the wheels and connecting rods so there was no visible means of propulsion. Each engine carried its number on an oval brass plate attached to these side panels. The company's title was also embossed on these

plates around the number. The engines were painted in an all over green livery.

The cars were 24ft long and were built by Messrs Starbuck & Company of Birkenhead. They were mounted on Mr JW Grover's patent flexible six wheel frames which enabled them to take extremely sharp curves without grinding the rails and at the same time made them safer on steep gradients. They weighed about two tons. Some of the early cars were open top but roofs and screens were soon fitted to protect the passengers from hot flying ash and cinders and fumes emitted from the engine chimneys. The cars carried a brown and cream livery.

The horse trams were quite small four-wheel double-deck cars. They were usually pulled by two horses but on gradients an extra lead or trace horse would be hitched to the front. At the terminus the horse would be unhitched and taken from one end to the other. Most tramway companies had about six or seven times as many horses as they had trams and one of the more important items in their budget was the price of hay. The speed of these horse trams was about 5mph.

The network expands

The Tottington line was opened in August 1883, the trams competing with the East Lancashire Railway line to Holcombe Brook which ran to the east of Tottington Road. It was said that the housewives of Tottington were so pleased at the arrival of the steam trams that they black-leaded the rails to mark the occasion.

When the line was open the Borough Engineer reported that the tracks were fairly constructed and equal to most lines he had seen in other towns. However, it soon became apparent that all was not as well as it seemed. First there was a lengthy dispute between the Council, the Company and the contractors regarding payment for the work. Then the steam locomotives proved not to be as efficient as at first thought being underpowered and unreliable. Breakdowns were frequent and the smoke and fumes were not being contained within the engine to the annoyance of the general public. The track too, which had been designed for horse trams, was causing problems as it was too light for heavy steam locos and tended to spread under their weight. The Bury to Kersal Bar section was relaid with new and heavier rails. In 1884 the Institution of Civil Engineers cited the state of the Company as an example of what could result from building a tramway on the cheap.

The lines to Tottington, Limefield and Heap Bridge were laid to the narrow 3ft 6in gauge and both standard and narrow gauge rails ran side by side in Market Street where they joined up to make a three rail mixed gauge track across the Market Place into Castle Street where there were separate entrances into the shed.

The track on the extension from Heap Bridge to Heywood was completed by September 1883 but because of a shortage of trams and a dispute with Heywood Council over widening the bridge, it was not opened until 8th March 1884. The new bridge was completed to its present width by the end of the year. During the time the work was taking place the line had been linked up with Rochdale via Sudden and was opened throughout on 30th May 1884. The branch from Heywood to Hopwood was opened the following month after a further dispute between the Company and Heywood Corporation.

Growing disenchantment

In 1884 the Company applied to Parliament for powers to increase the fares to passengers, to fix stages and to extend steam working to Stanley Street and the Walmersley Road section, but without consulting the Corporation. Heywood Council was also not pleased at the proposal to raise the fares. It was stated that the Company wanted to charge 4d to ride on the outside of the tram from Heywood to Bury or Rochdale, and 5d to travel inside. Heywood Council also opposed the Bill when it went to the House of Lords. The Corporation had the expense of appearing before a Committee and then an examiner to have all the undesirable clauses struck out. In this it was successful, Parliament deciding that the status quo must be maintained as set out in the 1881 order. Eventually, the company reduced the fares even below what it formerly had powers to charge.

By 1885 the six-wheel cars were not performing to their expected standard and so were replaced with more comfortable bogie cars, some of the six-wheel cars being converted to bogie cars by the Company.

The working of the steam tramways on the part of the drivers seems to have been very negligent in the early days. From newspaper reports of 1885 we read of a collision between a steam tram and a greengrocer's cart in Market Place, Heywood. The newspaper states that, "A mere youth was driving the tram engine at the time, and he stated that he could not bring his engine to a stand sufficiently soon to avoid a collision." Another report was of a 'tug of war' between two steam trams in Market Street when neither driver would give way and back up to the next passing loop. One tried to push the other but as the brake had been applied on the tram it would not move. Eventually one did back off but not before it had been seen by the public and duly noted.

By 1886 permission had been granted for Rock Street to be widened and steam trams were allowed to work the Limefield section. At the same time a triangular junction was laid in the Market Place involving only the narrow gauge tracks, making it possible for through running from Tottington to Limefield with the subsequent withdrawal of the horse trams.

Above: Heap Bridge over the River Roch which at this point forms the boundary between Bury and Heywood. *(TFC)*

Opposite page : A crowd gathers for the cameras as a policeman is photographed standing guard over the track-laying after the widening of Rock Street. *(TFC)*

Below : Tram number 45 with a Falcon trailer pictured in Heywood. *(TFC)*

The 1870 Tramways Act had contained clauses that were detrimental to the Company; the upkeep of its portions of the road was proving too costly and it was not prepared to lay out cash to improve the roads and rolling stock that could, in a few years, be purchased compulsorily by the Corporation. The Company applied to rid itself of more of its obligations to maintain the rolling stock and permanent way, again doing it without first obtaining the consent of the Corporation. The Parliamentary Committee of the Corporation endeavoured to meet the Company in every possible way compatible with the interests of the public but the Company refused to meet it except on terms detrimental to the ratepayers, leaving the Corporation no alternative but to oppose the Bill.

The state of the system continued to deteriorate and more complaints were received about the emission of noxious fumes and smoke coming from the engines. The track was not kept in good repair and the Corporation was compelled to ask the Board of Trade to enforce its powers to have these things rectified. The Board imposed fines on the Company for non-maintenance of the roads and the Corporation appointed three Inspectors to take note of any nuisances arising from the working of the engines and report them to the Council. Following this a Public Inquiry was held which was the first such Inquiry to arise under the Tramways

Act of 1870. The Board of Trade appointed a referee who reported that the allegations made by the Corporation were substantially true, that the roads were in a dangerous condition and that the Company was so insolvent as not to be able to carry out repairs. Ultimately, at the instigation of the President of the Board of Trade, the Tramway Company undertook to deposit in the Bank of England, to the credit of the Board of Trade, the sum of £3,000 by instalments, to cover the cost of repairs within the Borough, the repairs to be carried out by the Corporation. The state of the roads was then much improved.

However, in October 1887 the Company went into liquidation, the assets being taken over by a similarly named company omitting Manchester from its name.

The problem of fumes and smoke was more difficult to solve, appeals again being made to the Board of Trade. The Company's licence was renewed for limited periods of six and twelve months only between 1892 and 1894 and it was instructed by the Board's Examiner to modify its engines so as to cut down the amount of fumes that were being emitted and to stop oil dripping onto the roadway. It was also advised to have the engines and cars fitted with life protectors and emergency brakes. The Company took little or no notice. But things were not going to get any better.

Upper: About the turn of the century an unidentified narrow gauge car and trailer stand in the Market Place on the short-lived through service from Tottington to Rochdale. *(TFC)*

Lower : The crew of Beyer-Peacock car number 81 rest from their labours at the terminus on what is apparently the last day of steam operation in Heywood, 14th September 1905. It is not clear what part the lady in black played in the proceedings. *(TFC)*

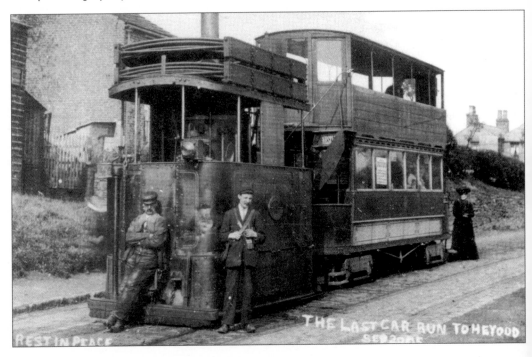

ELECTRIC TRAMS

A time of transition

By 1892 electric traction was beginning to be seen as the future method of propulsion and electric cars were already running in Halifax, Bristol, Dublin and Swansea, but the steam trams were still causing a nuisance in Bury. The tram service had now become, if not a necessity, then certainly a public convenience and to allow the six miles of track in Bury to be taken up was seen to be destroying a public utility. So, on this account, the Corporation and the Board of Trade dealt leniently with the Company. The Council felt that if the Company could not work the tramways with steam haulage without creating the nuisance it did, it should adopt a new mode of traction.

The feeling generally was that Local Authorities should own the tramways and work them with their own staff although the latter was not allowed under the 1870 Act. Manchester, Salford, Bolton and Huddersfield were already in possession of their tramlines and London, Leeds, Leicester and Cardiff had also decided to do this. Huddersfield and Bolton had been authorised under local Acts of Parliament to run their own systems and during that year many other towns sought similar powers.

In 1896 Bury Corporation built its first electric power station on a site at Crappers on Rochdale Road next to the present First Manchester bus depot, part of the building still standing today. In April of that year Mr Edmund Rothwell, the General Manager of the newly renamed Bury, Rochdale and Oldham Steam Tramways Company, informed the Council that, as the Corporation was at that time building an electricity power station, the Company was considering the use of electricity in place of steam. He asked if the Council would look with favour on the use of electricity and, if so, would they allow the use of overhead wires in the town, if the Corporation would supply the electricity and at what price?

The Council reserved its decision and formed a Sub-Committee, which visited Bristol to inspect the system there. At that time Bristol had a four and a half mile length of track with overhead wiring running out to Kingswood over quite steep gradients. The Sub-Committee could see the possibilities for the hills to be climbed in and around Bury and reported back to the Council that, in its opinion, there was no objection to the overhead wires being used. At the same time it suggested that the time was opportune for the Corporation to acquire the tramways, although no further move would be made in this direction for another two years. In 1898 the Council resolved that the Tramways Sub-Committee should, in the immediate future, consider the question of acquiring the tramways and the mode of traction to be used.

Later that year a Bill was put before Parliament to give the Corporation powers to acquire the steam tramways and to work them. The Steam Tramways Company petitioned to be heard against the Corporation obtaining these powers, but the Examiner disallowed this and the Bill passed the Select Committees of both Houses and received the Royal Assent. However, due to an agreement with the Water Undertaking, it was later decided to abandon the Bill.

Various options

In 1899 the Borough Surveyor was sent on a tour of several cities on the continent to inspect the working of tramways there, amongst the places he visited being Berlin, Brussels and Hamburg. At this time Hamburg was said to have had the best tramway system on the continent. On his return he pointed out to the Council that the overhead system of electric traction predominated, although in Berlin and Brussels it was supplemented by the use of secondary batteries in the city centre and thus there was no need for overhead wires spoiling the looks of the buildings. The Council was still concerned about the untidiness of the overhead and it was said that the wires looked as ugly as they were cheap. The use of accumulators, conduit and surface contacts was also discussed. Generally, the majority of towns and cities were in favour of the overhead system, but in one or two towns there was a strong feeling to the contrary. It was quoted that in America at that time there were 10,000 miles of overhead wires, but Washington and New York were examples of the electricity being supplied via underground conduits which was considered in most respects superior.

The Council also heard that at Wolverhampton a length of track had been laid using the Lorain

Surface Contact system and it was decided that a deputation should go there and inspect the working. However, it was not impressed and felt unable to recommend the system.

The Consultant's report

With tramway business taking up more and more time it was decided to set up a separate Committee to deal with it. The first Tramways Committee was appointed in November 1899 under the Chairmanship of Councillor Hutchinson, who at that time was also Chairman of the Douglas Southern Electric Tramways on the Isle of Man. The new Committee was instructed to prepare a system of electric tramways to be ready for working when the Steam Tramways Company's lease expired. Negotiations were also started with the outside authorities of Tottington, Radcliffe, Whitefield and Heywood to obtain their consent for Bury to run services in their districts. The Committee appointed Messrs Lacey, Clirehugh & Siller, Consulting Engineers, of 2 Queen Anne's Gate, Westminster to prepare a report.

On 19th January 1900 Mr Lacey met the Committee and together they inspected the routes to be covered by the new tramway system. In their report, the Consulting Engineers pointed out that unless small single deck tramcars were to be adopted, the 3ft 6in gauge was too narrow for larger cars designed for speed and comfort, and consequently the sections of that gauge must be widened and a heavier type of rail would be needed. Against this the cost of construction would be increased and sections of track would need to be interlaced or roads widened to provide for statutory clearances. However, the most important matter for consideration was that of intercommunication with neighbouring tramway systems, namely Manchester and Rochdale, which had both adopted the 4ft 8½in gauge and therefore they recommended that Bury should adopt the same gauge.

The consultants strongly emphasised that the success of electric traction depended upon rapid transit and frequent service, and that it was practically impossible to obtain good results on a single line unless a vast number of turnouts or passing places were laid down. After careful consideration they were of the opinion that an average of at least a 15-minute headway should be anticipated throughout the day upon all of the proposed tramways. For this it was recommended that 26 cars, each with accommodation for 41 passengers, should be acquired. The overhead method of electrifying the system was recommended although a conduit system had been considered and an estimate of the cost of this method had been included.

In addition to reconstructing the existing routes the consultants also proposed the following new lines:

'Along Moorgate and Bell Lane to the Workhouse.

Along Bolton Road to the Barracks.

From Manchester Road along Dumers Lane to a junction with the Radcliffe District.

Within the Radcliffe District from the Borough boundary on Dumers Lane along Bury Street, Cross Lane, Blackburn Street, New Road and Radcliffe New Road to Whitefield.'

These proposed tramways totalled over 17 miles of which more than 9 miles were within the borough. The use of the 4ft 8½in gauge meant that most of the track in the town had to be taken up and new track laid. The cost of the whole project was estimated at £318,473 if using the conduit system or £244,437 if the overhead system was used. Not surprisingly, the Committee resolved that the overhead system would be used as in the adjoining authorities.

The Tramways Committee proposed to have as much double track as possible to avoid delays at passing loops. With this in mind it suggested that in place of the interlacing track in Stanley Street, either the roadway would have to be widened or an alternative route would have to be found. The cost of the scheme caused a great deal of controversy in the town and Councillor Hutchinson, the Chairman of the Tramways Committee, pointed out in the local press that the estimate of nearly £300,000 to be spent on the new tramway system was the most important issue the town had to deal with apart from the domestic water supply.

In the provision of an electric tramway system, he went on, the Corporation was confronted with greater difficulties than at first sight appeared to be the case. Doubtless many ratepayers who had accepted the plans realised the hard facts that for two decades the town had been in possession of privately owned steam tramways and that these tramways were about to be substituted by a system of electric traction owned by the Corporation. He felt that these people had not taken the trouble to probe beneath the surface of the proposition before them, although they may have been consumed with wonder at the enormous cost of effecting the change. The estimate of over a quarter of a million pounds was to cover the whole initial expense of the undertaking. Of this £114,000 would be absorbed in street improvements.

The main ideas which had guided the Committee in drawing up these plans had been to so construct the system as to give some prospect of the undertaking returning a profit, that was to approach it from the point of view of a commercial undertaking and not one of seizing on it as a convenient opportunity for effecting town improvements here, there and everywhere. Street improvements would be carried out only where absolutely required to facilitate the working of the new system.

Further, the Committee would work by double lines wherever possible within the Borough, all the crossings and loops on the single lines would be within sight of each other and to avoid the present irritating stoppages at such loops the cars would run as frequently as possible. The cars would be conveniently wide, comfortable and comparatively speaking luxurious. Cheap workman's cars would run frequently so that workmen might live out in the country and be able to get to and from their work without difficulty and great expense. To facilitate the vehicular traffic in the main thoroughfares and avoid blockages, inward and outward routes would be provided for the Walmersley Road, Fairfield and Manchester Road sections. Councillor Hutchinson added that there were to be extensions to the tramways at Jericho, past the Barracks and along Dumers Lane, and the Whitefield section would be met by the Manchester electric tramways. If possible, an agreement would be made with the Radcliffe District Council for running powers that would enable a passenger to proceed from Bury to Radcliffe and on to Whitefield. They could transport people from the outside districts into the town and take people to the outskirts where buildings could be placed to avoid overcrowding. It was possible too that eventually both Bolton and the Rossendale Valley might be connected. All this would open a new vista of an agreeable mode of travelling throughout the country.

Negotiations were still going on to acquire the Steam Tramways Company and at a conference of interested local authorities held at Rochdale Town Hall on 18th February 1901 it was resolved that 'In view of the varying periods of the expiration of the powers of the Tramways Company, the various local authorities be requested to consider the question of the desirability or otherwise to acquire the undertaking of the company before such respective periods of expiration.'

Getting ready

By this time it had been decided to build a new tram shed, so the Council attempted to purchase the land where the Steam Tramway Company had its premises. In this it was unsuccessful, so it was decided to build at Whiteheads Bridge, on Rochdale Road between George Street and Foundry Street on land already owned by the Corporation and intended for a new Fire Station and a Municipal Model Lodging House to accommodate 252 men. It had previously been the site of an iron foundry owned by the Walker Brothers who built steam engines, both stationary ones for mills and factories and locomotives for use on rails. The land had been purchased in 1894 for £3,506 and covered an area of 6,453 square yards. The contract for building the depot was given to James Byrom of Elton, Bury.

Alderman Sykes laid the foundation stone on 23rd July 1902. In May 1987, during the demolition of the depot, the stone was rediscovered and is now in the Bury Museum in Moss Street. The inscription on it reads:-

> **THIS STONE WAS LAID BY**
> **ALDERMAN WILLIAM**
> **SYKES**
> **CHAIRMAN OF THE**
> **TRAMWAYS COMMITTEE**
> **23rd, JULY, 1902.**
>
> **Arthur W. Bradley**
> **Borough Engineer.**

The buildings were of bright red brick with stone facings. One track ran parallel to Foundry Street with fourteen tracks branching off at right angles, several of these lines having pits to give access to the under parts of the trams and connected by a single pit running the whole length of the building.

The repair and paint shops were at the front of the building and also had pits. Between the main building and the office block, which fronted on to Rochdale Road, there was an open yard that was used for storing permanent way materials and poles for the overhead equipment. The office block was a single-storey building consisting of a Manager's Office, a Clerk's Office, a Men's Mess Room and toilets and store rooms. The cost of constructing the depot was £9,839. The depot was completed in March 1903, and was designed to accommodate 48 cars.

Up to now the planning and construction work had been overseen by the Borough Engineer, but now that the opening of the system was drawing near it became necessary to appoint a manager to oversee the running and administration. So Mr William Clough was appointed to the position of Tramways Manager from 14th April 1903. Mr Clough was a native of Bury and was currently employed as the Chief Clerk in the Borough Engineer's Department. He was to carry out such duties temporarily from that date until such time as the Steam Tramway Company's undertaking was acquired, his pay being £1 5s 0d per week. He had joined the Borough Surveyor's Department in December 1892 at the age of 19. Only two days before Mr Clough's appointment was announced, Eastbourne Corporation inaugurated the world's first municipal motor bus service between the Railway Station and Meads.

During that month the Tramways Committee made several decisions regarding the running of the tramways. First, it decided to use pre-printed tickets and punches for the collection of fares. An offer by Messrs A Williamson of Ashton-under-Lyne to loan the Committee three ticket punches was accepted and at the same time an order for 200,000 tickets to be printed by them was placed at a cost of 4d per 1,000. Numerous requests were received from advertising agencies to display advertisements on the trams and to be printed on the backs of the tickets. The Committee approved

Interior view of the new George Street depot. *(MMT)*

of advertisements being displayed both internally and externally and also on the tickets but no agreement was made with any of the agencies at that time.

During 1903 the firm of Johnson-Lundell Electrical Traction Company Limited asked the Council if it would consider the use of their surface contact system. After a lengthy discussion it was decided that the Company should be allowed to lay an experimental length of track on Rochdale Road, between Henry Street and King Street, provided no expense was incurred by the Corporation. However, the firm could not lay the equipment in the time stipulated in the agreement and the contact system was never put down.

A few days previously some members of the Tramways Committee had had the opportunity to travel on a tram throughout from Liverpool to Bolton. The South Lancashire Tramway Company's system had, a few days earlier, bridged the last remaining gap with the opening of its line from Haydock to Hindley. To celebrate the occasion the Company organised a convoy of six special cars to travel over the route and civic dignitaries and managers of a large number of tramway undertakings were invited to ride on the cars. The convoy left Liverpool Pier Head at 9.15am arriving at Bolton Town Hall at 2.07pm. A 30-minute break was taken at Atherton to inspect the South Lancashire Tramways depot and power station.

Afterwards, Alderman Sykes said that before long he hoped to see tramcars marked 'Liverpool Corporation' opposite the Derby Hotel in Bury. There was only a short section between Bolton and Bury required to make that desirable state of things possible.

The Fairfield route

With trams on order and agreement not yet reached on the takeover of the steam trams, it was decided to construct the short route from Moorside to Fairfield first. Although it had originally been

A period scene in Moorgate as tram number 2, the Milnes bogie car which carried the Board of Trade inspectors along the route on 3rd June 1903, stands at the temporary Moorside terminus of the Fairfield route soon after the service began. The view would not be recognisable now as Moorgate has been re-aligned and the Swan Hotel and the Bury Coffee Shop in the background are long gone. *(MMT)*

In a similar scene to that on the previous page, Milnes 4-wheel car number 24 is pictured in Moorgate when working on the Fairfield route. *(ADPC)*

planned for the route to terminate at the Workhouse (now Fairfield Hospital) it had later been decided to economise by cutting it short at what was then the end of the built up area near where the M66 Motorway now crosses the road. The Bury Board of Guardians had asked the Council on several occasions to reconsider this as at the time there were at least 650 persons in the Workhouse. The Board felt that with the amount of official and public business that was carried out there the Council was obliged to run a service at least to the Workhouse and at the same time visitors would have easier access, saving them the walk up the hill, besides increasing the revenue received. After much discussion, the Council altered its decision and agreed to lay the line to the westerly boundary of the Workhouse at a point approximately where Rectory Lane is now, near the George and Dragon public house. At that time there were fields either side of the road along that stretch.

Work began on the Fairfield route in November 1902. The line was single track with passing loops at the Grapes Inn, Pine Street, Ferngrove and Martin Street. As the Corporation was not yet in possession of the Steam Tramway sections, the Fairfield line was isolated from the Corporation

tram depot on Rochdale Road and so a temporary tram shed was built at the Fairfield terminus. It held three cars on a single line and had facilities to carry out repairs. When the line was later extended through to Bury centre the trams were able to use the main tram shed and the temporary shed at Fairfield was dismantled.

When the first three trams were delivered, they were assembled at the temporary shed ready for use on the route. They had large plate glass windows with draped curtains sliding on brass rails and each car had its own clock. To support the overhead wires, welded taper poles and welded taper brackets were used. On double track sections the trolley wires were carried by span wires and on single track by bracket arms the poles being set in the kerbs. The current was supplied to the overhead wires through section boxes placed at half mile intervals. The boxes were fitted with four switches and a telephone and electricity was supplied by underground cables. The cost of the one and a half miles of route on the Fairfield section was £10,000.

On Tuesday 2nd June 1903 several test runs were made along the route by the new trams. The next day the Board of Trade Inspectors, Majo

At the other end of the route tram number 17 of the same batch stands at the Fairfield terminus watched by two little girls. The crenellated George and Dragon Inn in the background is virtually unchanged although the Fairfield Workhouse to the right of the picture is now the much enlarged Fairfield Hospital. *(ADPC)*

Druitt and Mr AP Trotter, met the Tramways Committee Chairman and Deputy Chairman, Alderman Sykes and Councillor Spencer, and rode over the route in car number 2 to inspect the track. Apart from a few minor details it was found to be fit for service.

At 5pm that evening at Moorside, the Bury Corporation Tramways were officially opened by the Mayor. Councillor Roger Duxbury. Then, to the cheers of the large crowd, cars number 1 and 2, gaily decorated for the occasion and filled with civic dignitaries from the town and the surrounding area, travelled up to Fairfield. Cheering crowds lined the route and houses were decorated with flags and bunting. On arrival at Fairfield the cars were given an enthusiastic welcome by the people who had gathered there and from inmates of the Workhouse who were standing in the grounds. The cars then returned to Moorside and the route was declared open to the public. The guests were then invited to a tea in the Derby Hotel and many toasts and speeches were given during the evening. A toast to the health of the Mayor was proposed and replied to and the evening's proceedings were brought to a close by singing the National Anthem.

During the evening numerous journeys were made to Fairfield with many hundreds of people travelling on the trams, eager for an early ride. In fact, when the takings were reckoned up, it was found that 3,049 people had travelled the route,

making the money collected for the four hours that evening £12 14s 1d, each person paying 1d for the journey from Moorside to Fairfield and 1d back. The scheduled tram service actually started the following Friday morning, 5th June 1903.

The service proved so popular that in August the Tramways Committee had to ask the Police Superintendent to have a constable on duty at Moorgate to assist in regulating the queues during Saturdays and Sundays because of the large number of passengers boarding the trams during certain hours.

The end of the steam trams

While work was progressing on the Fairfield route, the Tramways Committee was busy negotiating with the Steam Tramways Company. The Directors of the Company were approached and a number of meetings took place with them to reach a settlement on the payment for the tramways and their equipment. In March of that year, at the half yearly meeting of the Company's shareholders in the Grand Hotel, Manchester, Mr John Coomer, the President, mentioned that Bury and Rochdale proposed to run the trams in the Heywood district. The authorities had expressed a wish that one date should be mutually agreed when they should give notice of their intention to purchase the property of the Company. He said that the directors did not at that time know the purchase price that would be

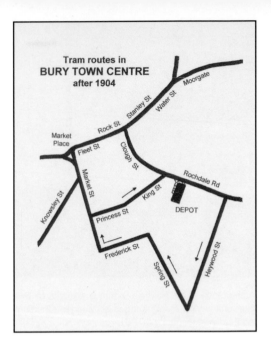

Tram routes in
BURY TOWN CENTRE
after 1904

any sections whenever they thought fit for the purpose of reconstruction.

On 24th February 1904 the sections were taken over by their respective local councils. In Bury the end came on the evening of Sunday 10th July 1904 when the last steam tram left the centre of Bury for Tottington. Without any ceremony, the end of an era came to a town that had been served by these trams for over twenty-one years. Most of the townsfolk were pleased to see them go. They had not been the favourites of other road users with their noise, fumes and oil that had dripped onto the carriageway. The local papers reported that 'Auld Lang Syne' and other songs had been sung by passengers making the last journey.

Under the agreement it was provided that the lines in Whitefield should be included in the arbitration, and that such additional sum should be paid as the arbitrator might consider fair in consideration of the Company agreeing to sell these lines seven years before being compelled to do so at the end of their lease. The District Council of Whitefield declined to proceed on these terms and the tramway in their district was not sold at that time but continued to be owned by the Company and worked as a steam tramway.

The arbitrator who had been appointed to value the Steam Tramways Company's plant, materials and premises commenced his work on 31st May 1904 at the Surveyors' Institute in London and continued until 6th June when the proceedings were adjourned as no agreement could be reached. Mr Graham Harris was then appointed as a referee by the Board of Trade. The local authorities had offered £123,784 for the Company, the Company in return asking for £205,675. The referee's decision was £162,675 of which Bury Corporation had to pay £45,546 5s 6d as it was also responsible for the sections in Tottington and Unsworth. The scale of the referee's over-generous valuation of the Company's assets became evident when the sale of the depots and equipment realised only £6,286. The steam locos had been valued at £398 each but when sold they were found to be of little use and the price they brought ranged between £18 and £50 each. The tramcars were valued at £130 each but when sold only realised £4 to £7 each. When the Corporation re-laid the track with heavier rail the old rails were taken out but even these were found to have little value and when sold brought in very little cash.

fixed. When the authorities gave their notice, the Company would appoint a valuer and if possible terms would be amicably arranged, but if not it would be necessary to apply to the Board of Trade for a referee to fix an amount that would be binding on both vendor and purchaser. The Chairman added that so far as the negotiations had gone the Company had been met by the authorities in a straightforward and honourable way.

To allow the local councils to carry on with their construction of the permanent way it was agreed that on 31st July 1903 the individual councils would acquire the sections within their areas and work them. However, this was found to be impossible as it was illegal. On 9th November a conference of local authorities, held in Rochdale, decided that under the 1881 Act an arbitrator should be called in. The Board of Trade was requested that proceedings should start at once and Sir Frederick Bramwell was appointed as arbitrator. At a further meeting held in Rochdale Town Hall on 22nd December the Steam Tramways Company and the Corporations reached an agreement which covered, amongst other things, the working of the tramways during the arbitration and until the completion of the sale.

The agreement ran from 1st August 1903 and all traffic receipts and expenditure from that date were the responsibility of the purchasers. The purchasers were at liberty to take possession of

The Bury depot was put up for auction along with two other Company depots at Rochdale and Royton, the auction taking place in the Thatched House Hotel, New Market Place, Manchester on 24th January 1905. After some hard talking between Mr Kenyon, the auctioneer for Messrs Rushton, Son & Kenyon of Manchester, and Colonel Wike, representing the 1st Battalion of the Volunteer Brigade of the Lancashire Fusiliers who owned the Drill Hall on the adjoining land, the Corporation were able to obtain £50 for the site. It was estimated that the fittings alone were worth £250 and the depot as a whole was expected to have made £5,000! The steam tram shed was demolished in 1905 and the Castle Armoury was extended in 1906 to its present size using the stone.

The Bury Rochdale and Oldham Steam Tramways Company had been the second largest steam tramway undertaking in Britain. At the time of its dissolution it ran a total of 30 route miles with 91 locomotives and 81 cars. One of the Company's locomotives was preserved. This was number 84, a Wilkinson standard gauge type built by Beyer Peacock at Gorton in 1886. When the Company was wound up it was one of three sold to the Ince Foundry at Wigan. In 1955 it passed to the British Transport Commission for preservation and was initially put in store at British Railways' Crewe Works. It later moved to the Dinting Railway Centre and eventually ended up in the Manchester Museum of Science and Industry where it was last known to be stored in a broken-down condition, although it is doubtful if there are enough parts left for it ever to be resurrected even if it still exists.

Locomotive number 84, built by Beyer Peacock at Gorton in 1886, was the only tramway locomotive to survive into preservation. On the demise of the steam tramways it passed to the Ince Foundry at Wigan where it is photographed in later years working as a shunter. It is now in the possession of the Manchester Museum of Science and Industry. *(TFC)*

BEYOND THE BOUNDARIES

Tramways in Radcliffe

The town of Radcliffe is situated some two and a half miles to the south-west of Bury. It is mentioned in the Domesday book as Redeclive and with the industrial revolution became important for coal mining and cotton spinning. It joined with Bury in 1876 but in 1894 broke away to become an Urban District.

Unlike most towns in the area Radcliffe never had either horse or steam trams and at one time it was intended that the town would eventually own and run its own tramway system. In 1900, by the Radcliffe Urban District Council Tramways Order, authorisation was given for the construction of a system of tramways in Radcliffe and neighbouring Whitefield which also gave Radcliffe full operational powers in its own right, although these were never taken up. In its 1901 Act the South Lancashire Tramways Company had been empowered to construct any lines authorised by the Radcliffe and Whitefield Orders which had not yet been built. However, if the Company merely obtained running powers in Radcliffe and Whitefield and did not purchase or lease these systems, then Radcliffe Urban District Council was to have running powers in Little Lever and also over those lines of Farnworth Urban District Council and Whitefield Urban District Council for which the Company possessed running powers.

The Whitefield Urban District Council Tramways Order authorised the electrification of the part of the Broughton to Bury line situated in Whitefield together with a branch from Whitefield along Radcliffe New Road to the Radcliffe boundary. The Radcliffe Urban District Council Tramways Order authorised eight miles of line from Stopes through Radcliffe and along New Road to the Whitefield boundary and along Cross Lane and Dumers Lane to the Bury boundary. In addition it authorised a further section from Radcliffe along Black Lane and Ainsworth Road to the junction with the Bury and Bolton Road at the 'Three Arrows' and along the Bury and Bolton Road for the one and a half miles that lay in the Radcliffe area. This latter stretch of road was significant as it bridged the gap between Bury and Bolton and would eventually allow through running between these two towns. As the South Lancashire Tramways line from Farnworth through Little Lever to Stopes was never laid none of that Company's powers in the area was ever exercised.

As time went on, Radcliffe Council came to the conclusion that running its own tramway might not be such a good idea so in January 1903 negotiations opened with Bury Corporation and in the May a provisional arrangement was reached between the two authorities for laying down and working a tramway system in Radcliffe. By a further agreement dated 24th March 1904 Bury agreed to lease the Radcliffe tramways and operate them for a term of thirty years. The estimated cost of the Radcliffe system was £37,220 although the actual cost came out at £41,568.

It was decided that the first section to be laid should be from Radcliffe Bridge to Whitefield to give Radcliffe people convenient access to Manchester. The contractors started the work in October 1904 and finished it within one month. The overhead was completed on Friday 31st December and the Radcliffe Tramways Committee was so enthusiastic at getting the line open that a trial run was arranged for the following afternoon when several hundred people gathered to see the car glide into the town. It left Whitefield a few minutes after 3pm and arrived at Radcliffe Bridge seven minutes later driven by the Tramways Manager, Mr Clough. With him was Councillor JH Lund, the Chairman of the Radcliffe Electric Committee. Two more journeys were made that afternoon and the following Tuesday morning Major Druitt of the Board of Trade inspected the line and found it fit for service. The speed allowed on this section was 14mph in New Road, 8mph between the Bridge and the Fountain in Stand Lane and 4mph round all curves and through facing points.

The formal opening was on Wednesday 5th January 1905 when members, officials and guests of Radcliffe Urban District Council, Whitefield District Council and Bury Corporation assembled at Whitefield District Chambers. At 3pm two gaily decorated cars stood at the end of Elms Road for the occasion. The party boarded and set off with Councillor G Mills of Whitefield Council driving the first car. When crossing the boundary it was handed over to Councillor Slingsby of Radcliffe Council who then drove it to Radcliffe Bridge. The

Management and civic dignitaries gather round car number 33 as it stands at the Bury and Radcliffe boundary in Dumers Lane at Hardy's Gate Bridge. The date is 24th June 1905 and the occasion is the completion of the Radcliffe tramways and the linking up of the two systems. *(TFC)*

second car was driven all the way by Councillor und. At the bridge a large crowd thronged the footpath to witness their arrival. After a second journey had been made, the invited guests from both cars adjourned to the Assembly Rooms in the Boars Head Hotel where refreshments were served. The service then commenced and ran for several hours doing a brisk trade. The takings for the first week were £62 2s 10d. The fare from Whitefield to Radcliffe Bridge was one penny.

Work progressed on the other sections and the route from Radcliffe Bridge to Stopes was opened on 18th April, the short section along Black Lane to Mill Street (later renamed Miller Street) following a month later on 5th May. Negotiations then started with Bury on linking the two networks along Spring Lane, Cross Lane, Bury Street and Dumers Lane to the Borough boundary at Hardy's Gate Bridge where the line would join up with a short spur which Bury had laid in the previous year as part of the Manchester Road scheme.

The final link-up with the Bury Tramways took place on Saturday 24th June 1905 when two cars decorated with flags, coloured paper and banners carrying the words 'Success to the Radcliffe Tramways' in large red letters hanging on each end left Bury at 2.30pm and travelled down Manchester Road to Whitefield, then along Radcliffe New Road, over Radcliffe Bridge and on to stop outside the Council Chambers. Here the Councillors and their guests boarded and set off for Hardy's Gate Bridge. On the route many of the houses had flags flying from their windows and at Top-o'-th'-Cross bunting was strung across the roadway. A short ceremony took place at the boundary after which the cars returned to Radcliffe and a tea was provided at the Technical School.

The Radcliffe system consisted of five and a half miles of track, being wholly single line with passing loops.

Ramsbottom

Ramsbottom Urban District Council had been considering some form of local transport since the last decade of the 19th century when the Lancashire Light Railway Company proposed to construct a tramway from Blackburn to Manchester via Rawtenstall, Ramsbottom and Bury. Then in 1901 the Turton, Tottington, Ramsbottom and Rawtenstall Light Railway was promoted to operate routes from Tottington to Turton Bottoms and to Edenfield via Holcombe Brook and Ramsbottom. Neither proposal materialised and in 1903 the Council sought and obtained powers to construct tramways within the District. These were from Edenfield through Stubbins and Ramsbottom to Holcombe Brook and through Shuttleworth to Ramsbottom, the latter line being conditional upon the construction of a bridge or a tunnel to cross the railway at Ramsbottom Station.

In October 1904 Ramsbottom wrote to Bury suggesting building a tramway from Tottington terminus through Greenmount, Holcombe Brook, Ramsbottom and Stubbins to Edenfield and on to Rawtenstall with another line from Edenfield through Shuttleworth to Walmersley. Bury Tramways Committee then suggested an alternative scheme for a route along Brandlesholme Road, Longsight, Holcombe Brook and Ramsbottom to Stubbins, together with a second from the Bury boundary on Walmersley Road at Bass Lane through Shuttleworth to Edenfield and the boundary between Ramsbottom and Rawtenstall.

Bury was currently preparing its Bill to extend the Bolton Road section to the Radcliffe boundary to allow through running between Bury and Bolton together with various other extensions in the Borough and the Tramways Committee decided to incorporate Ramsbottom's suggestions in it. The cost of these proposed extensions was estimated at £194,000. This aroused some resentment amongst Bury ratepayers with a public meeting being called in the YMCA on Wednesday 28th December 1904. The Chairman was a Mr Ramsden, who said that there was plenty of room for criticism of the Tramways Committee, that these extensions were to cost £194,000 and that, as Bury was undoubtedly a non-progressive Borough, trade conditions generally did not warrant the Tramways Committee embarking upon such a large expenditure as the scheme would involve if it went through. He considered it unreasonable to ask the rate-payer to find such a large amount of money for the scheme. It was felt that the Tramways Committee should show that there were prospects of reasonable return on the money spent and if this were done the ratepayers would view the scheme more favourably. A resolution was passed that the Tramways Committee were not to continue with the Ramsbottom scheme until the ratepayers had given their consent. The following year Bury Corporation applied for powers to construct a tramway within Ramsbottom from the Borough boundary at Walmersley through Edenfield to the boundary with Rawtenstall at the Quarryman's Arms.

Nothing materialised with either proposal and Ramsbottom never got its tramway system although a depot was built on Stubbins Lane with an inscription on the front of it saying 'RAMSBOTTOM TRAMWAYS'. However, in 1913 Ramsbottom District Council inaugurated a trolleybus service on the route between Holcombe Brook and Edenfield.

The Heywood tramways

Heywood is a small town some three miles east of Bury which became a Municipal Borough in 1881. When the Steam Tramway Company was dissolved Heywood Corporation purchased thirteen locomotives and cars and ran its own steam tram service for a time, a tram shed being built in the old Towns Yard off York Street.

In November 1904 the Town Clerk of Bury received a letter from the Town Clerk of Heywood raising the question of working the proposed Heywood Tramways. Meetings were held with Heywood Corporation and later with Rochdale Corporation and, on 28th April 1905, members of Bury, Heywood and Rochdale Tramways Committees met and drew up an agreement in respect of through running of trams from Bury to Rochdale via Heywood. This differed from the Radcliffe agreement in that Heywood would build and own the lines but, instead of simply leasing them it would also maintain them and allow Bury and Rochdale to run the service, paying a proportion of their working expenses and taking a share of the revenue, in effect becoming a joint operator.

In November 1904 Heywood Corporation purchased 13 trams from the steam tramway company to work its operations in the borough. The service commenced on 20th December 1904 and was withdrawn on 20th September the following year, allowing Heywood to become the last municipally owned steam tramway in the country and also the shortest lived. One of the locomotives, still carrying its former company number 63, is pictured in the Market Place showing its new ownership on the side panel. *(TFC)*

On the last day of steam trams in Heywood another of the locomotives purchased by Heywood Corporation, Beyer, Peacock-built Wilkinson type engine number 81, stands at the Rochdale boundary at Marland end to end with a Rochdale car. *(TFC)*

The agreement was for a minimum of three years with Heywood then having the option, at six months notice, to run its proportion of the service and purchase six trams from Bury to do it. To operate the service Bury ordered six more balcony cars from the Brush Electrical Engineering Company Ltd on Mountain and Gibson trucks with Westinghouse electrical equipment which were numbered 36-41.

Work started on the reconstruction of the Heap Bridge to Heywood section in mid-August and the route was terminated at Summit while work progressed between there and Heywood Centre. Most of the track materials for this section were delivered by rail to the sidings at Prettywood, near Heap Bridge. By this time Heywood had become the last municipality to operate steam trams in Britain, continuing in Heywood until 20th September 1905.

During the discussions between Bury and Heywood Councils some controversy was brought about by several alterations which were made and put into the draft agreement and by 10th October a final working agreement still had not been finalised between the two Corporations. The completion of the line between Heap Bridge and Summit was imminent and the Tramways Committee was anxious to get it running. Mr Clough was instructed to make the necessary arrangements for working the line between these two points as soon as it had been inspected by the Board of Trade and the Electricity Department was asked to supply the current until terms could be arranged with Heywood Corporation. At a meeting on 7th November between the Mayor and Town Clerk of Heywood and Bury's Tramways Committee Chairman and Tramways Manager, it was agreed to start the cars running as soon as possible as far as Pilsworth Road. A few days later, on 13th November 1905, an agreement between Bury and Heywood Corporations was completed and signed whereby a through service between the two towns was secured.

A trial trip with a Bury car ran through to the Heywood Reform Club at midnight on Thursday 16th November. Amongst those on the trip was the Mayor of Heywood, Councillor Hall, the Chairman of Bury Tramways Committee, officials of the two Corporations and representatives of the contractors.

On the morning of Friday 17th November Colonel Druitt, the Board of Trade Inspector,

arrived at Bolton Street Station at 9.45am when he was met by the Mayor of Bury and other officers and dignitaries and conveyed to Heap Bridge in a special car. At Heap Bridge they were met by the Heywood contingent led by the Mayor and Colonel Druitt went over the whole of the completed track and passed it fit for service. The speed limit was set at 14mph except for Heap Bridge and Market Street where the limit was 10mph. In the evening the Heywood section was formally opened by two decorated cars bearing the motto 'Success to the Heywood Tramways'. They were driven from Bury depot to Heywood Market Place, arriving about 8pm and were welcomed by a large crowd of people waiting to see the Mayor of Heywood drive the first official electric car into the town.

Public working of the tramway between Heap Bridge and Pilsworth Road commenced that evening and the next week trams started running through to Heywood Town Centre from Tottington. The Heywood Parish Church to Hopwood section was inspected by Colonel Druitt on 1st March 1906 and was opened for service the same day.

Extensions in Radcliffe

In April 1905 Radcliffe Council raised the question of extending the tramway to include those parts of the proposed system that had not yet been built. Powers had been obtained for these lines in the original Radcliffe Urban District Council Tramways Order, but they had been allowed to lapse.

In May Radcliffe deposited a Bill in the following session of Parliament for the requisite powers. The lines concerned ran along the Bury and Bolton Road from the boundary between Bury and Radcliffe at the Jolly Carters to the boundary between Radcliffe and Bolton at the Coach and Horses at Breightmet and an extension of the line from Mill Street (now re-named Miller Street) along Black Lane to meet the Bury and Bolton Road at the Three Arrows.

At the same time Bury Corporation placed a Bill before Parliament for extensions to the tramways within the Borough. These were:

'From the terminus at Wellington Barracks along Bolton Road to the Borough boundary at the 'Jolly Carters' to join up with the proposed Radcliffe extension.

Before the new extensions in Radcliffe were opened, number 20, a Milnes car dating from 1903, stands on New Road at the Radcliffe Bridge terminus while the conductor turns the trolley ready for the return journey to Black Lane. *(ADPC)*

To celebrate the opening Bolton Corporation car number 36, suitably decorated and illuminated for the occasion, ran between Bolton and Bury during the evening of 16th May 1907. The new services did not open to the public until four days later. *(STA)*

From the terminus at Limefield along Walmersley Road to the Borough boundary.

From the terminus at the Fairfield Workhouse to the Borough boundary at Smethurst Hall, Jericho.'

An extension to the depot was also included to be built on the land that had been left vacant since the depot was built in 1903. Also in the Bill was an application to use the existing tramway in Clough Street for passenger traffic which hitherto had only been used for cars coming into service from the depot. Bury's Bill was opposed by the Lancashire and Yorkshire Railway Company on the grounds of abstraction of traffic and by the Bury Brewery Company because of alleged interference with the businesses of two licensed houses in Clough Street. Before reaching the House of Commons agreement was reached with both objectors so the Bill was passed by the House of Commons Unopposed Bills Committee and received the Royal Assent on 20th July 1906.

A second agreement was then drawn up with Radcliffe Urban District Council dated 7th December 1905, whereby the Corporation of Bury agreed to take a lease on the extensions. With the important exception that Radcliffe should contribute one half of any loss on the working of these tramways, the second agreement was identical to the first. Work on the Radcliffe lines and the section in Bury from the Barracks to the boundary was carried out simultaneously.

Lieutenant Colonel Druitt inspected the lines on the morning of Thursday 16th May 1907 and apart from a few minor points declared it fit for service. Then at 2pm that afternoon a special car carrying representatives of Bury Council and their guests left the Market Place and travelled along Bolton Street and Bolton Road to a point just beyond the Barracks where Councillor Hall was presented with an inscribed Rose Bowl on an ebony plinth and a pair of silver scissors to cut the ribbon at the Radcliffe Boundary. Here they were met by representatives of Radcliffe District Council who had arrived from Radcliffe by a special car. A short ceremony had already taken place near Miller Street to mark the opening of the extension along Ainsworth Road to the Three Arrows.

The cars were then driven over the boundary by the respective chairmen and after being photographed went on to the Bolton boundary at Breightmet where the Bolton Corporation

representatives were waiting surrounded by a large crowd of people. A red, white and blue ribbon was stretched across the track as a barrier between the two towns. Councillor Hall opened the formalities by cutting the ribbon over the line from Bury and Alderman Miles cut the ribbon over the line from Bolton and pronounced the route open. They then drove their respective cars over the boundary to the opposite side. The whole party then proceeded in the cars to Horwich where they were met by three waggonettes and taken for a drive around Rivington Pike and Lever Park. Later, in the evening, the party returned to Bolton for a dinner in the Pack Horse Hotel on Bradshawgate. In the evening an illuminated Bolton car toured the Bury lines.

The route was not used until the following Monday 20th May as there were a few defects that Lieutenant Colonel Druitt wanted to have put right. The opening of these two miles of track, called by some people 'The Golden Key' joining the East to the West, made it possible to travel by tram right through from Liverpool to Littleborough Summit and within a few weeks Bolton cars could be seen passing through Bury on special trips to Heaton Park and Belle Vue Manchester.

A few months later a request was made for a further extension from Stopes through Little Lever to join up with the tramways in Farnworth but after inspecting the route with its narrow roads and sharp corners the request was turned down and there would be no further lines built in Radcliffe.

A period of consolidation

The Bury system, including Heywood and Radcliffe, would now remain stable for a number of years. The overhead system was maintained by a gang of about eight men who at first pushed their ladders and equipment around on a hand cart with the words 'BURY CORPORATION TRAMWAYS' painted in script lettering on the sides. Later a tower wagon was purchased drawn by two horses hired from the Cleansing Department when the wagon was to be used but in February 1906 the Tramways Department acquired its own horse called Bob from the Cleansing Department at a cost of £35.

An agreement was made with the Cleansing Department whereby the watering of the street o lay the dust was transferred to the Tramways Department. For this purpose an electric water car was purchased from the local firm of Mountain and Gibson, with the same truck and electrical equipment as the six cars (36-41) built for the Heywood extension. The Cleansing Department paid the Tramways £200 per year for this service which included the supply of water which was obtained from the reservoir in Clarence Park on Walmersley Road. The water was contained in a cylindrical steel tank with a capacity of 1,800 gallons seated on a steel underframe, the pressure required to spread the water the full width of the street being obtained by an air compressor driven by a 3hp electric motor. In addition to spraying pipes, rail flushers were also provided. The tank, compressor and other accessories were enclosed in a body fitted with a canopy roof extending the full length of the vehicle. The dashes, fenders, platforms and steps were of the ordinary car type. On either side of the body was a tool locker set under the tank. The tram was powered by two 25hp motors and cost £790. In the first year of its operation 873,000 gallons of water were distributed on the streets of Bury. It was also used for carrying tools and materials for track work and snow clearing and was later fitted with carborundum blocks between the wheels for grinding out the corrugations in the rail surface.

To house the extra cars needed for the Heywood and Radcliffe routes the depot was extended to accommodate an extra 27 cars, stables, tower wagon shed and workshops, until this time only temporary provision having been made for workshops. Work started on 1st March 1907 by excavating an area 80ft by 160ft. Four entrances were made in the new building and two more were made in the wall of the old building on George Street. Nine tracks were laid inside the new building, all the work being carried out by the permanent way gang. The depot was then capable of accommodating 71 cars, and was completed in October 1908.

The workshops comprised a machine shop, a blacksmiths shop, a sand and salt store, an armature repair shop and wiremans room and two store rooms. The workshops were in a two-storey block fronted by Foundry Street. At the same time a stable and harness room and tower wagon house was built in the open yard between the tram shed and the office block near to the entrance from Rochdale Road. The stable was at the other end of this building and between the two was the harness room with a hay loft over the top.

At this time it was also decided to weld the rail joints instead of using fishplates. This made the running of the cars much quieter and there was less wear on the wheels.

The electric water car based on a standard Mountain and Gibson truck is pictured in the depot in later years. *(ADPC)*

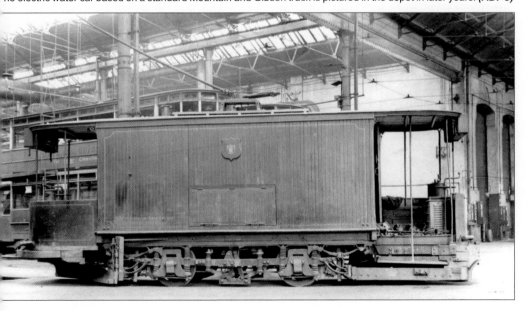

At the end of March 1907 the number of cars in stock was 41, consisting of 14 73-seat bogie cars and 27 56-seat single-truck types. Six more 56-seat single-truck cars were built in 1907 for the Bolton Road and Radcliffe extensions. Mountain and Gibson supplied the trucks, the United Electric Car Company of Preston built the bodies and top deck covers and the Westinghouse Company of Trafford Park, Manchester, fitted the electrical equipment and magnetic brakes. The automatic sanding equipment was supplied by Messrs M Cummins of Manchester and the cars were assembled in the depot by the depot staff. The cost of these cars was £720 each. They took the numbers 42-47. Three more identical cars (48-50) were built in the same way during 1910 and a further four (51-54) were completed in 1913.

The existing office in the town centre was now too small for the number of staff using it, so in 1908 the ground floor of the Castle Buildings in the Market Place was leased. The accommodation was re-arranged to provide a waiting room, cash office, general office and a Manager's office. In the basement a room was fitted out for the drivers and conductors to eat their food at meal breaks. These offices had previously been occupied and leased by the Union Bank of Manchester Ltd and had been built in about 1874. In January 1916 the building was put up for sale and was purchased by the Corporation, the first floor housing the general offices and the upper two floors being leased to a number of small businesses. The offices remained in the Castle Buildings for many years but in 1980 were moved into smaller accommodation in the new transport interchange.

Heywood to Rochdale

In April 1908, negotiations were opened on the terms of a new operating agreement with Heywood Corporation. The current agreement, which was for three years terminable on six months notice by either side, was due to expire on 13th November that year. Agreement could not be reached on the terms of a replacement so, once again, Heywood decided to go it alone. In the Parliamentary sessions of 1909, Heywood Corporation promoted a Bill in which powers were sought to run cars into Bury and Bury was offered facilities to run cars to Heywood Market Place and to Hopwood. At the same time Bury Corporation promoted a

Consolidation Bill in which powers were included to run a service of cars through Heywood and on to Rochdale with both Heywood and Rochdale to have facilities to run into Bury. Bury Corporation felt that if a through service of cars between Bury and Rochdale could be instituted, it would be to the convenience of the public and of mutual benefit to the three authorities concerned.

The tramways portion of the Heywood Corporation Bill and the Bury Consolidation Bill came before a committee of the House of Commons on 16th June 1909 and an agreement was concluded between the three Corporations of Bury, Heywood and Rochdale which became the Heywood Corporation Act 1909. The new agreement dated from 1st August 1909 and was terminable by Heywood Corporation at the end of ten years and at subsequent recurring intervals of ten years, and provided for through running between Bury and Rochdale. Bury were to manage and operate the section between Heap Bridge and Hopwood, Rochdale to manage and operate the section between Heywood town centre and the Rochdale boundary at Marland and each of the three Corporations would receive the fares and pay the costs within their respective areas. This of course meant that Heywood was still an operator in its own right although taking no active part, a situation which was to be a thorn in the side of both Bury and Rochdale, and indeed Manchester as well, in the future. Through running between Bury and Rochdale commenced on 1st August 1909.

Also in 1908 agreement was reached with Salford whereby a sum of money was paid annually in respect of their lengths of track between Unsworth Boundary and Whitefield Railway Station and also between Goats Gate and Whitefield Railway Station.

On 22nd April 1908 Councillor (Colonel) John Hall resigned as Chairman of the Tramway Committee. He had been a member of the Committee since November 1902 and was elected Chairman in November 1903. At that time the undertaking had been at the most critical period of its existence when the policy adopted meant the success or otherwise of the system, negotiations with the Steam Tramways Company were proceeding unsatisfactorily, whilst those with Heywood Corporation were at a deadlock. However, within three months, an agreement had been reached with the Steam Tramways Company and shortly afterwards the negotiations with Heywood Corporation were amicably settled. Under Councillor Hall's guidance the tramway system had been created, developed and placed on a sound basis and his resignation was an irreplaceable loss to the undertaking,

Looking to the future

For a number of years tramway operation in Bury stayed relatively static although elsewhere there was steady development in other modes of transport. At a meeting of the Local Government Officers' Association held in Bury Technical School in Broad Street in January 1913, Mr Clough delivered a lecture on tramways in which he gave an historical sketch of the horse, steam and electric tramways in Bury, interesting observations on tramways in general and his thoughts on the future. He said that out of the 296 tramway undertakings in the country, 174 were owned by local authorities and the other 122 by companies. He went on to mention that during the second half of 1912 it was seriously put forward that a less expensive means of transit had been found in the motor bus which had recently become very much cheaper than before. In London there had been a road war between the motor buses and the tramways. He continued, "So far the victory appears to have been with the motor bus judging by the injury which has been done to the tramways in London and District. In the provinces there might not be all the advantages so particularly favourable to the motor buses competing with the tramcars, even in Bury and District". In conclusion Mr Clough referred to the trackless trolley system: a motor bus driven by electricity obtained from overhead wires. It was put forward as a means of supplying transit facilities in sparsely populated districts as a feeder to existing tramways by connecting up lengths of road along which it would not pay to put down a permanent way. In the neighbouring district of Ramsbottom a length of trackless trolley line was to be constructed and its future would be closely followed, because it would be one of the earliest systems run on its own and not run in conjunction with some existing tramway system.

At the Annual Conference of the Municipal Tramways Association held in Sheffield in September 1913, the President, in his address, pointed out that in the accepted order of things, electric tramways should, by this time, have gone through half their life, if those of their predecessors, the horse tramways and the steam tramways, were taken as a guide. London trams, he said, were already a burden on the rates. He considered that for most of the municipalities, when a new route was needed it was a question of whether to extend the tramway, use trackless cars (Trolleybuses) or use motor buses.

If trackless cars or motor buses were used another question would arise: 'Are the roads suitable to carry these vehicles?' Sheffield had equipped a section of its track for a trackless car to run on for the conference delegates to inspect. They also had for their inspection a motor bus, one of ten which they were using as a feeder service to the tram routes.

Walmersley and Jericho

In Bury's 1906 Bill powers had been granted to extend both the Limefield and Fairfield routes to the Borough boundaries but at the time there was not enough housing along either route to justify the cost and the powers had been allowed to lapse. Now, however, due to development beyond both termini, it was decided in November 1913 to apply to the Board for a Provisional Order to construct a double line from Limefield to the New Inn at Walmersley and a single line from Fairfield Workhouse to Smethurst Hall, Jericho.

The biggest problem was on the Walmersley route just after the Limefield terminus where the road made a steep descent to the narrow bridge over Pigs Lee Brook. The brook was culverted and the roadway was raised by 11ft and widened and straightened at a cost of £6,061. Work started during April 1914 and on the much simpler Jericho extension in the October. Lieutenant Colonel Druitt inspected both extensions on 23rd February 1915 and expressed himself as satisfied and said that trams could start running at any time. Owing to the war, the Department was short of staff and found it difficult to run the services through to the new termini straight away. However, within a fortnight the new extensions were in regular use. These extensions were the last lengths of track to be laid in the Bury system, bringing the total route length to 12½ miles.

A new tower wagon was needed to replace the existing one which had been in use since 1906, so in 1913 the Department purchased a motorised tower wagon. It was a three and a half ton Leyland with a 30hp engine and cost £700. It proved itself valuable in reducing the time taken for the wiremen to travel from where they were working carrying out normal maintenance, to where a break in the overhead may have occurred.

In July 1914 Mr Clough drew up a list of places where he thought shelters were needed for intending passengers. These were at Whitefield, Hollins Brow (Blackford Bridge), Cemetery Lane (now St Peters Road), Parkhills Road, Tottington terminus, Moorside junction and Chesham Road. It was felt by some Councillors that a shelter was needed at Heap Bridge but after much discussion it was decided not to put one there. The shelters were made of timber and were about 10ft by 6ft with glass in the upper panels to allow people to see the trams approach. Seats were placed around the inside but no doors were fitted. They lasted for many years, the last being at the old Tottington terminus which was demolished in 1980.

Bury trams in Radcliffe. On the left UEC car number 47, new in 1907, leaves the terminus at Stopes on its journey to Bury. Seen below at the Three Arrows on a working to Black Lane is number 35 which entered service in 1905. Although they did supply top covers for several Bury cars this was the only complete tram built by the Bury firm of Wilson and Stockhill, mainly from spare parts from the Corporation's workshops. It was withdrawn in 1933. *(both MMT)*

WAR AND PEACE

The First World War

The First World War started on 4th August 1914, bringing with it shortages and increased prices. Due to the high cost of steel, only the most urgent repairs were made to the track during the next five years. By early 1915 staff shortage was proving quite a problem for the Department as by 31st March that year 102 of its men had enlisted into His Majesty's Forces and the Manager reported to the Tramways Committee that owing to these men being called up he was unable to maintain a reasonable service on the routes and therefore it would be necessary to employ women conductresses. This was agreed and within a month women were being employed in this work. There were at one time 80 women working on the trams during the war.

The Corporation made a decision that men going in the forces would have their wages paid less any pay given to them by the Army or Navy.

In June 1915, the Manager informed the Tramways Committee that he had been requested to sit on the Local Munitions Committee. The Council resolved that the Manager be empowered to act on this Committee and that the Chairman and Deputy Chairman of the Tramways Committee, along with the Manager, be authorised to place the tram depot, machines and tools at the disposal of the Munitions Committee if deemed necessary and to render every assistance possible. By August there was an acute shortage of munitions for the Military Forces and an agreement was reached regarding the making of shell cases at the depot. This work carried on until the end of hostilities when the Corporation requested the Bury and District War Munitions Committee to vacate the premises they occupied at the depot. Notice was served on the 20th November, 1918.

The war brought many wounded soldiers to Bury. The Infirmary and Holly Mount Convent at Tottington, and during the latter years the Workhouse at Jericho, were used to treat these soldiers for their injuries and to convalesce and the Tramways Department made special arrangements for the men to travel on the trams free. Wounded soldiers wearing Hospital Blue uniforms were allowed to travel at half the usual fare and those unable to walk without aid of crutches were allowed to travel free. A supply of tokens was given for travel on trams and in some cases passes were issued, these being reviewed every month. Arrangements were also made for parties to visit numerous places, the trams being provided free of charge.

In May 1917 the Admiralty applied to the Corporation for the 'loan' of Mr Clough to assist in the work of the Shipyard Labour Department as a voluntary Establishment Officer. The Corporation placed his services at their disposal and accordingly he spent the greater part of his time as an Inspecting Lost Time Officer. Whilst with this Department he introduced a timekeeping scheme and in this capacity he regularly visited the docks around the country, only returning to Bury from time to time to control the operations of the tramways. Later in the war Mr Clough went on the Board of Trade Tramways Committee and was placed in charge of the Priority Section, which granted certificates for the supply of materials to various tramways.

On Monday 3rd June 1918 the London Gazette published a list of people receiving awards in the King's Birthday Honours List. Bury's Mayor, Councillor James Hacking, received a knighthood and became Sir James Hacking. Also in the list was Mr Clough who was appointed a Member of the Civil Division of the Order of the British Empire (MBE) for his services in connection with the war when he was Organising Officer of the Bury Munitions Board of Management. Mr Clough went to Buckingham Palace on 22nd October, when he was invested with the MBE by King George V. The same month Mr Clough was appointed Secretary of the Municipal Tramways Association.

On Monday 11th November 1918 the Armistice was signed in a railway coach at Compiegne in Northern France, bringing the war to an end. To commemorate this, the tramway service was closed at 2pm.

Under new management

The same day that the Armistice was signed, after serving with the Corporation Tramways Department for over 15 years and with the Corporation as a whole for some 26 years, Mr Clough gave notice that he wished to resign his position. He had been responsible for the inauguration of the electric tramway system and the conversion of the steam tramways to electric traction. He had seen the tramway system grow from a very small beginning to its position as the premier profit-making undertaking of the Corporation. He always had the satisfaction of knowing that he was the person responsible for the installation of the electric tramway system in his native town. At that time the Bury system was regarded as one of the most successful of the medium sized tramways and he left it on a sound basis.

Mr Clough's successor was Mr Frank Buckley who was then the General Manager of Wigan Corporation Tramways. Previous to that he had been Assistant to the General Manager of Salford Corporation Tramways where he had been for ten years. He had started his career with Wigan Corporation in September 1912 when he was appointed Traffic Manager of the Electricity and Tramways Undertaking and when, in July 1914, the Electricity and Tramways Department was split up he became General Manager of the new Tramways Department. His salary with Bury was £500 per year.

Peace Day Celebrations

To celebrate the armistice on 'Peace Day' in May 1919, the Tramways Department had one of its bogie cars decorated with red, white and blue flags, ribbons and stars. Some 3,000 electric light bulbs were used in the decorations so that during the hours of darkness it was an illuminated spectacle. At each end was the word 'PEACE' with over it the letters 'GVR' and above these Saint Edward's-type crowns, all the shapes having bulbs in them. The flags included the Union Jack and the Stars and Stripes. Two big stars were fixed to the stair rails, one at each end. On one side were the words:-

> SUCCESS CROWNS SACRIFICE.
> DUTY NOBLY DONE.
> 1914 1918

And on the other side:-

> VICTORY ACHIEVED.
> HONOUR SUSTAINED
> 1914 1918

At the same time as the tram was traversing the system, the town centre offices of the Tramways and Electricity Departments were also decorated to be illuminated at night. Again the word 'PEACE', the letters 'GR' and a crown were part of the decorations.

During football season special trams were run from Bury to Starkies (Redvales Road) which was the tram stop used by supporters going to Gigg Lane Football Ground. Football specials were also run from Whitefield and Radcliffe to Starkies. After the matches the trams lined up in readiness to take supporters to their respective destinations. When more popular matches were played and Bury's trams were not expected to cope with the volume of passengers, Salford City Tramways provided cars for journeys between Whitefield and Bury. For the movement of these large crowds to Gigg Lane and to relieve traffic congestion in the Market Place a special tramway siding was laid in Haymarket Street along the western side of Kay Gardens in time for the 1924/5 season. The football specials continued to be run, later by buses, until 1972.

During 1925 Bury took delivery of its last tramcars, 12 years after receiving the previous batch. Numbers 55-60 were built by English Electric on Burnley maximum traction bogies with electrical equipment by GEC and seated 80 passengers in a fully enclosed body, the first of its kind in Bury, although several of the older cars were later rebuilt to the same standard.

The Heywood to Middleton line

Ever since taking over its portion of the Steam Tramway Company Heywood Council had nursed ambitions of extending the Hopwood branch to Middleton, but it was not until 1925 that it was considered seriously. Then, on 9th August 1925 Manchester, Oldham and Rochdale Corporations jointly took over the operations and rolling stock of the Middleton Electric Traction Company which in addition to tramways had been operating a bus service between Heywood, Hopwood and Middleton since March 1921. Heywood and Manchester Corporations entered into discussions and Manchester agreed to construct a line from the Middleton system at the junction of Rochdale Road and Hollin Lane to join up with the terminus of the former steam tramway branch at Magdala

Car number 60 was the last tram to be built for Bury. New in 1925 it was one of six bogie cars supplied by English Electric. Three of the batch were sold to Bolton in 1943 but 60 remained at Bury until the end of tramway operation, being pictured here at Walmersley in 1947. *(MMT)*

Street, Hopwood and also to take over any outstanding debts and commitments.

Delays then ensued while Heywood and Middleton Councils obtained the necessary powers under the Heywood and Middleton Light Railways Order 1927. Work started on 16th May 1927 and after being inspected by Colonel Trench on behalf of the Board of Trade a through service from Heywood to Manchester started on 19th May 1928, the Bury to Hopwood service being cut back to Heywood on the same day with Bury providing one car on the new service. Bury car number 30, which had gained a totally enclosed top cover in 1926, was rebuilt with a new EMB truck, GEC 50hp motors and compressed air track brakes to work on the new service alongside Manchester's lightweight Pilcher cars.

This was the last extension of the Manchester Corporation Tramways system and was to be short-lived, the line being replaced by buses in April 1934, although Bury's operation ceased earlier with the final withdrawal of trams between Bury and Heywood in February 1933. Its completion stored up a can of worms for the future as, with Manchester taking over the running rights from Bury between Hopwood and Heywood, this meant that three operating areas met in the town centre.

Services were then revised with the Heywood to Bury and Heywood to Rochdale services being linked across Heywood on 13th July 1928 to provide a through service between Bury and Rochdale which had not existed since the demise of the Steam Tramway Company.

The Middleton Company's bus service over the route between Middleton and Heywood was taken over by Manchester Corporation and was withdrawn when the new tramway opened.

A joint tram service with Salford City Tramways numbered 63 commenced between Bury and Manchester (Deansgate) via Whitefield on 4th January 1926.

The Middleton Electric Traction Company operated a bus service between Heywood and Middleton from March 1921, duplicating Bury's tram route between Heywood and Hopwood. The service was taken over by Manchester Corporation in May 1928 and cut back to run between Hopwood and Middleton until Manchester trams were extended to Heywood in 1928 when it was withdrawn. In the picture a green and white Daimler Y-type stands with its crew in Heywood town centre. *(MMT)*

Bury car number 30 was rebuilt with a new truck, new motors and compressed air track brakes to work the Bury to Manchester service alongside Manchester's much more modern Pilcher cars. It is seen here at Blackley while running on the new service. *(MMT)*

EARLY MOTOR BUSES

Skirmishes on the boundary

By 1922 Ribble Motor Services was becoming very active in the area, expanding its operations south and east from its Preston base and running services in the more rural districts beyond the boundaries of the larger towns. The long-running saga of the turf wars between Ribble and the South Lancashire tram-owning municipalities is complex, but it should be remembered that at that time the Councils not only issued the licences but acted as judge, jury and executioner. They were naturally very protective of their own interests, often refusing the Company's applications out of hand or imposing onerous conditions. The resulting number of appeals, counter appeals and injunctions, repeated across the country, was one of the reasons that the 1930 Road Traffic Act took road service licensing away from the local authorities and put it into the hands of independent Traffic Commissioners, thereby establishing a more level playing field.

In all this Bury was only involved at the margin and locally the main push came in November 1923 when Ribble applied for a network of inter-urban services, among which were Bury to Blackburn and Bury to Burnley via Edenfield and Rawtenstall. The Tramways Committee refused both applications and on 3rd May 1923 representatives of Ramsbottom and Bury Councils met and agreed that Ramsbottom should run a service between Edenfield and Bury's tram terminus at the New Inn at Walmersley.

Ramsbottom then started a service running between Rawtenstall and Walmersley, but Ribble threatened it with an injunction to restrain its operation, so from 1st September 1924 Ramsbottom transferred its rights and vehicles to Rawtenstall Corporation which had powers to operate beyond its boundary. Then a week later, on 8th September, Rawtenstall extended the service at both ends to create a through service between Bury and the Burnley boundary. From 21st November 1924 the service was operated jointly by Bury, Ramsbottom and Rawtenstall, although at that time Bury did not have any buses to run its share of the operation.

In August 1925 Ribble again applied to run services from Bury to Blackburn and Burnley and also to Edgworth via Tottington and to Bradshaw via Ainsworth and Harwood. All these applications were refused.

Bury's first bus routes

Although Bury Council was satisfied that its tramway network was adequate for the town, the same could not be said for those members of the public living away from the tracks, notably in the west of the borough in Walshaw and Elton where pressure was growing for some form of transport. In July 1925, mindful that other operators were waiting in the wings, the Tramways Committee decided to operate a bus service along Crostons Road and Walshaw Road and Mr Buckley, the

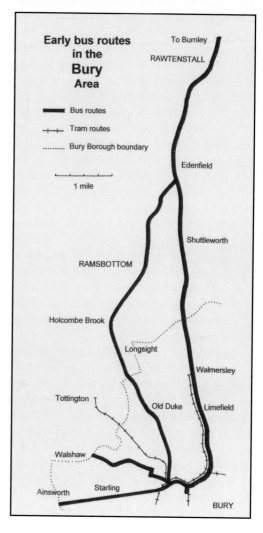

Early bus routes in the Bury Area

━━━ Bus routes
┼─┼─┼ Tram routes
.... Bury Borough boundary

1 mile

To Burnley
RAWTENSTALL
Edenfield
Shuttleworth
RAMSBOTTOM
Holcombe Brook
Longsight
Walmersley
Tottington
Old Duke
Limefield
Walshaw
Ainsworth
Starling
BURY

Manager, was instructed to obtain tenders for two one-man operated buses. The order went to Leyland Motors who supplied two C7 chassis with 26-seat front-entrance bodies painted vermilion and cream, carrying the fleet numbers 1 and 2 respectively. They arrived on Saturday 12th September 1925 and during the following week were put on show to the public in Bank Street where they were also inspected by the Tramways Committee. Having received approval from the Ministry of Transport, the Walshaw bus route started a week later on Friday 18th September, appropriately numbered 1, although at that time route numbers were not displayed on the buses.

The drivers collected the fares by using pre-printed tickets and hand punches in the same way as the tram conductors. The fare from Bury (Kay Gardens) to Walshaw War Memorial was 3d and at that time the speed limit on the road was 20mph. In November of that year it was decided to alter the route so that the buses travelled from Crostons Road along Wood Street and Pine Street (now Harvey Street) to Walshaw Road in order to get better penetration of the Elton area. A third identical bus was ordered, numbered 3.

While this new service satisfied the aspirations of residents along Walshaw Road, there were other important roads in the west of Bury which were unserved. So, on Friday 6th March 1926, two more routes were introduced starting from Bury Bridge, one along Ainsworth Road to the Black Bull at Starling numbered 2 and the other along Brandlesholme Road to the Old Duke numbered 3, the two routes being interworked. Through booking on the trams to Bury was possible at Bury Bridge. From 19th March the Starling route was extended to Ainsworth. The new services required two buses and a further pair of Leyland C7s, identical to the existing three, were delivered taking the numbers 4 and 5.

By December 1925, the Tramways Committee was considering the question of running buses to neighbouring towns and Mr Buckley reported that steps were then being taken by the Municipal Tramways Association to secure legislation giving Local Authorities the necessary Parliamentary powers. Ramsbottom Urban District Council suggested running buses from Ramsbottom to Bury via Holcombe Brook, Longsight and Brandlesholme Road. Application was made to Parliament and by the Ramsbottom Urban District

Council Act of 1926 the Council was empowered to run buses within the district and, with the consent of the Ministry of Transport and of the local authorities concerned, outside the district, and also to enter into running agreements with other operators.

So, on 18th November 1926 a service was introduced between Edenfield and Bury via Ramsbottom, Holcombe Brook and Brandlesholme Road. This was operated solely by Ramsbottom until 1927 when Bury obtained powers to operate up to five miles outside the Borough. A pooling arrangement was agreed between Bury and Rawtenstall Corporations and Ramsbottom Urban District to the effect that the routes from Bury to Rawtenstall via Ramsbottom and via Walmersley should be operated jointly in equal proportions. This came into force on 28th November 1927 and on that date a further service started between Bury, Rawtenstall and Burnley Summit via Walmersley although the section of route between Rawtenstall and Burnley Summit was not included in the pooling agreement. At Burnley Summit the buses made connections with Burnley Corporation Tramways. Bury gave the services route numbers; 3 via Brandlesholme Road, absorbing the Old Duke journeys and 4 via Walmersley Road. Some time in the early thirties the numbers were swopped over with 3 being used for Walmersley Road and 4 for Brandlesholme Road. There doesn't seem to have been any reason for this and nobody would have noticed at the time as none of the three operators displayed service numbers. In fact neither Rawtenstall nor Ramsbottom ever numbered their services.

To work its proportion of the pool routes Bury ordered four Leyland PLSC Lions with Leyland 30-seat bodies which were unusual for the time in having dual entrances incorporating features of both front and rear entrance design, including the rear emergency exit set in the centre of the rear panelling, normally found only on front entrance bodies. They were numbered 6-9. With an eye to the future the Committee extended the order by a further two buses which became 10 and 11.

In May 1926 neighbouring Rochdale Corporation had started a service linking its tram terminus at Rochdale Cemetery with the Bury trams at Jericho. This was far from convenient as it meant that passengers travelling between the two towns had to change twice. So on 19th

Three of Bury's first buses are pictured on this page. Above is number 5 (EN 3000), one of two 26-seat Leyland A13s which were bought in 1926 for the one person operated Starling and Old Duke services. The bus was withdrawn in 1932 and passed to the Express Transport Company of Bury as a lorry.

By 1929, as traffic grew, larger crew-operated vehicles were needed and the two buses on the right are typical of the more modern buses coming into service at that time. The upper photograph shows number 14 (EN 4312), a Leyland Lion LT1 with a 31-seat two-door body by Charles H Roe of Leeds standing with its driver outside the depot. Number 14 lasted through the Second World War before going out on loan to St Helens Corporation. It was finally withdrawn in 1948, ending its life as a showman's lorry.

The lower picture is of number 17 (EN 4315), a Roe-bodied Dennis EV, at the Walshaw terminus. The large letter C was intended to distinguish Corporation buses from the similar red buses of other operators. *(All DBC)*

December 1927 alternate journeys were extended at either end to run between Bury and Rochdale. The service would later become 19 when Rochdale numbered its services in 1931. Then on 7th January 1928 a new service 6 was introduced along Manchester Road and Radcliffe Road to the Radcliffe boundary at Warth.

Although Harry Orr, trading as HG Orr and Sons of Little Lever, was already running a service on the route, in January 1929 Radcliffe District Council asked Bury Corporation to run a bus service between Radcliffe and Manchester. Bury suggested that the tramway service between Stopes and Whitefield along Radcliffe New Road should be abandoned and a bus service run in its place. While agreeing to consider this, Radcliffe proposed that in any event Bury Corporation should run a through service of buses between Stopes and Manchester via Chapel Field (Stand Lane). Bury stated that at that time they could not run buses over the suggested route, but on 4th February, whilst both Councils were still deliberating, Salford Corporation stepped into the gap and introduced a service from Salford (Greengate) to Stopes via Whitefield, Radcliffe New Road (Goats Gate), Radcliffe Town Centre and Bolton Road. Then on 18th February it extended its Eccles to Besses o' th' Barn service along Higher Lane, Ringley Road and Stand Lane to Radcliffe Bridge. Agreement was then reached between Bury and Radcliffe and on 3rd June 1929 Bury introduced a service between Whitefield and the 'Three Arrows', replacing the trams with the exception of the peak hour extra journeys. On 28th April 1930 Bury and Salford finally started the long-requested express service from Stopes to Manchester, although it was to be short lived, being withdrawn two years later on the orders of the Area Traffic Commissioner following a complaint from the LMS Railway under the 1930 Road Traffic Act, of which more later. Orr soldiered on but he eventually sold out to Manchester, Bury and Salford Corporations.

On 14th January 1929 the General Manager, Mr Buckley, resigned having been appointed Manager of the Norwich Electrical Tramway Company, taking up his duties on 1st March. The position was advertised at a salary of £650 a year with two annual increments of £50 to a maximum of £750. A short list of six applicants was invited to attend an interview on 11th March and Mr Andrew Fenwick, Engineer and Assistant Tramways Manager at Dundee was appointed to the post. A native of Perth, Mr Fenwick had been employed by Dundee Corporation Tramways Department since 1911.

On 12th August 1929 an express service was introduced between Bury and Rochdale via Jericho. This was short-lived and on Monday 21st October it was withdrawn and replaced by an express service between Bolton and Rochdale via Breightmet, Bury and Heywood, operated jointly by all three Corporations. It ran every half hour, the fares being 1/4d single and 2/- return between Bolton and Rochdale.

On 19th December 1927 a service had been introduced between Bury and Stockport (Dialstone Lane) via Manchester. Initially, the service was run by Salford, Manchester and Stockport Corporations, but from 6th October 1929 Bury took part in the operation. Bury's buses ran through from Stockport to Burnley Summit, although passengers making that journey had to re-book in Bury as through-booking was not available.

With Stockport, Manchester, Salford, Bury, Ramsbottom and Rawtenstall all operating red buses at that time, Bury's single deck buses had boxes set on the roof over the front destination indicator with a large letter 'C' denoting that it was a Corporation bus.

Later, in August 1930, the Bury to Burnley Summit section was extended through to Burnley Cattle Market. Ribble took legal action and the extension was declared *ultra vires* because there was no working agreement clause in the Burnley Corporation Bill. It was abandoned on 31st March 1932 and cut back to Rawtenstall. A pooling agreement between Bury, Ramsbottom and Ribble dated 31st December 1931 defined the boundaries of the area and put an end to uneconomic competition by making Ribble buses available to local passengers without restrictions.

To work these new services a total of eight buses was delivered during 1929. These were four Leyland LT1 Lions with Roe 31-seat two-door single-deck bodies numbered 12-15 and four Dennis EVs with similar bodies numbered 16-19. All eight had the 'Edinburgh' style open rear platform which was supposed to obviate the need for a rear emergency door, but Bury still had one fitted.

A DECADE OF CHANGE

The 1930 Road Traffic Act

The growth of bus services in the late 1920s was beginning to put a strain on the existing licensing system authorised by the Town Police Clauses Acts of 1847 and 1849 and designed to deal with hackney carriages, whereby prospective operators had to obtain licences from each individual local authority along the proposed route. This had not mattered much so long as the bus routes were only short feeders to the trams, but as services became longer and began to cross municipal boundaries it started to cause problems.

The main purpose of Herbert Morrison's Road Traffic Act was to streamline the licensing procedure by taking it away from the multitude of local authorities, each with its own independent transport policy, and concentrating it into a number of Traffic Areas presided over by Government appointed Traffic Commissioners. The intention was to simplify the process and bring consistency to the decision-making. So far as the passenger industry was concerned it covered the issue and renewal of Road Service Licences, Public Service Vehicle Licences and Driver and Conductor Licences. Trams and trolley buses were not covered by the regulations.

Bury came within Area C, the new North Western Traffic Area with its headquarters at Sunlight House in Manchester. The Chairman of the Commissioners was Mr (later Sir) William Chamberlain who had been Oldham's General Manager from May 1918 until April 1925 and who resigned from his position as General Manager of the Belfast Corporation Tramways to take up the post.

All existing operators now had to apply for licences to continue the services they were already running. However, transitional regulations were issued on 9th February 1931 under which all vehicles and services operating on that date were allowed to continue running until such time as the applications for new licences could be heard and determined. The Minister of Transport made it clear, however, that permission to continue an existing service did not carry with it any rights, and the Traffic Commissioners would not be placed under any obligation when they came to consider the grant of the substantive licence for these services.

Established bodies, such as local authorities, other operators and the railway companies, were able to object to applications, even if the services had been running for a considerable time, although they would have to put up convincing arguments in support of their objections. Generally, town services operated by the local councils continued unchallenged, the majority of objections being against the longer distance inter-town services, particularly the expresses, where the railway companies seized the opportunity to reopen old arguments and get a second bite at the cherry.

Bury was involved in three express services, only one of which was part of the Manchester network and this, the Bury to Stockport service, was split in Manchester City Centre being curtailed at Cannon Street on 25th October 1931, at the same time being re-routed via Bury Old Road and Cheetham Hill. The others were Bolton-Bury-Rochdale which survived unchanged and Bury-Burnley which was curtailed at Rawtenstall in March 1932.

The SELEC scheme

Following the implementation of the 1930 Road Traffic Act, discussions took place on the subject of a Joint Municipal Passenger Transport Board for South East Lancashire and East Cheshire, known as SELEC, the brainchild of Manchester's General Manager, R Stuart Pilcher. In 1931 representatives of Ashton, Bolton, Bury, Leigh, Manchester, Oldham, Rochdale, Salford, SHMD, Stockport and Wigan met to discuss broad principles of a merger. Leigh and Wigan soon withdrew as they had little common interest with the rest of the group, but Manchester continued to host a series of conferences on the subject.

There were, however, two main stumbling blocks to agreement; fears of the loss of local influence over services and fares, and worries about how the different outstanding capital debts would be treated. One by one operators withdrew. Bury pulled out in 1935 leaving only Manchester, Salford and Oldham to go it alone. However, despite encouragement from the Ministry of Transport during 1936, the three remaining operators decided not to promote the necessary Bill.

Nothing more came of the idea although a series of conferences of all the municipal operators in the area plus Ribble, North Western and Lancashire United and the LMS and LNE Railways took place the following year which again came to nothing and it was not until 34 years later that the 1968 Transport Act would create the Passenger Transport Authorities and Bury Corporation Transport would be no more.

The North Garage

By the beginning of 1930 Bury was operating 19 buses and four more arrived in April and May. These were Bury's first double-deckers; Leyland Titan TD1 models with 48-seat bodies by Massey Brothers of Wigan which were numbered 20-23. All these buses were garaged in the tram shed and, with more on order for additional services which were planned for the future, space was already at a premium. So it was proposed to build a garage on land then belonging to the Electricity Department on the north side of Rochdale Road opposite the tram shed.

The Borough Engineer submitted plans for a building with an estimate of the probable cost which was to include a wash plant and after careful consideration it was resolved that the scheme be approved and submitted to the General Purposes Committee and that the Borough Engineer should obtain tenders for the erection of a garage.

A month later the Town Clerk received a letter from the firm of Wilson & Ingham Limited offering for sale their weaving shed and warehouse in Derby Street for use as a garage. The Borough Engineer, the Manager and members of the Tramways Committee visited the property but were not satisfied and the Committee turned down the offer.

The land on Rochdale Road cost the Tramways Department £600 and the building of the garage, store shed and boundary wall another £7,500, including a grant from the Ministry of Transport. The garage was in use by February 1932. The roller shutter doors were replaced by single sliding doors in the late 1940s, these being removed and motorised folding sliding doors fitted in August 1964. At the same time the No 2 bay entrance was widened to allow easier manoeuvring of the longer 30ft buses on entry and exit.

Expansion

In March 1930 Mr William Lees of Radcliffe approached Bury Corporation with a view to selling his business. This consisted of five buses operating on three routes; Radcliffe Bridge via Black Lane to the Three Arrows on the Bury and Bolton Road, Radcliffe Bridge to Farnworth via Stoneclough, and Whitefield to Blackford Bridge via Unsworth and Hollins. The Tramways Committee proposed that the Corporation should acquire the firm jointly with the Lancashire United Transport and Power Company Limited of Atherton, the General Purposes Committee confirming this on 21st March. It was decided that Bury would run the Unsworth route and Lancashire United would operate the Radcliffe to Farnworth route, the Three Arrows route being abandoned as Bury was already running a parallel tram service under the Radcliffe agreement and in fact some journeys were already being covered by buses.

No buildings were involved in the transaction and Bury acquired only one vehicle from the Lees fleet, a Leyland A13 coach which received fleet number 24. It carried the registration number BN 4190 and was painted blue and yellow with the wording '*Whitefield - Unsworth - Blackford Bridge*' on the sides. The service, which was given the number 8, was operated by Bury Corporation from 24th March 1930 still using this vehicle. It only stayed with the Corporation for about three months before being withdrawn and was the first bus that Bury Corporation Tramways had owned that was not registered in the Borough. The Corporation also acquired one of Lees' drivers, Mr Tom Allison. On 8th May Bury's service 6 was extended from Warth to Radcliffe and linked to the former Lees Radcliffe-Farnworth service by now operated by Lancashire United. Numbered 25, both operators ran on the new route.

Due to the restricted width of roads in the Freetown area the Corporation had only been able to provide a single tram track in the inward direction and for many years the residents had been asking for an equivalent outward route. Eventually, it was decided to provide this with motor buses for a trial period, so on 11th July a service began running along Market Street, Frederick Street, Spring Street, Heywood Street and Bond Street to Wash Lane. Later it was rerouted along Market

Street, Wellington Road and Heywood Street. Neither route was successful and the service was withdrawn on 28th November 1931.

A new joint venture by Bury Corporation and Ramsbottom UDC during 1930 was a long-distance express service from Heywood to Blackpool which began on 19th July and ran on Tuesdays, Wednesdays, Saturdays and Sundays. The starting point was the Cenotaph at Heywood and the route went via Bury (Kay Gardens), Holcombe Brook, Ramsbottom, Stubbins and Edenfield to Blackpool (Talbot Mews). The return fare was 4/6d from Heywood and 4/- from all other picking up points. Children under 14 years were allowed to travel at half fare and passengers could book in advance. Ribble Motor Services was not happy and succeeded in having the service declared illegal and being withdrawn.

On 1st September 1930 buses took over from trams on the Bury-Radcliffe-Stopes route. Buses on the new service 6 ran every 15 minutes with additional buses and trams at peak periods.

Bury Council thought it would be a good thing if they could come to an agreement with Bolton Corporation and Harry Orr's Motor Services of Little Lever for the Bolton buses to turn back at Little Lever Market Place and for Bury buses to go through to that point and applied to Little Lever District Council for permission to extend the bus service from Stopes to the Market Place. Having in mind the congestion in Market Street, the Little Lever Streets Committee resolved that this should not be granted. The Chairman of the Little Lever Committee was of the opinion that Bury would not have asked for this extension had it not been substituting buses for trams and it would have been satisfied to keep the terminus at Stopes. It was better for Little Lever to keep the terminus on their side. Later, when agreement was reached for joint services between Bolton and Little Lever, there was a stipulation that no other buses should be allowed to go into the village until Bolton Corporation and Mr Orr had been given an opportunity to consider the matter.

One of the buses purchased for evaluation during 1930 was number 31 (EN 4723), a Crossley Alpha with Vulcan 32-seat two-door body. Although the model was popular elsewhere this example only lasted seven years, passing to the Borough Surveyor's Department and then to the War Department in 1940. *(MMT)*

In February 1931 Bury applied to the Traffic Commissioners for licences for the following services which it was already operating:

Bury-Walshaw (1)

Bury-Ainsworth (2)

Bury-Ramsbottom-Rawtenstall (3)

Bury-Rawtenstall-Burnley (4)

Whitefield-Radcliffe-Three Arrows (5)

Bury-Radcliffe-Little Lever (6)

Bury-Chesham (7)

Blackford Bridge-Whitefield (8)

Little Lever-Radcliffe-Manchester (17)

Bury-Rochdale (19)

Bury-Stockport (20)

Bolton-Bury-Rochdale (23)

Bury-Radcliffe-Farnworth (25)

There were also Sunday morning journeys on the tram services which were operated by buses. Note that the Rawtenstall services are still referred to by their original numbers, but some time later the numbers would be transposed.

Having decided to experiment with buses from other manufacturers than Leyland, orders were placed during 1930 for a total of seven vehicles with different combinations of chassis and body. Fleet numbers 25-31 were allocated, but with manufacturers having a variety of delivery times, buses turned up in a different order over the next 12 months. First to arrive in the October were three single-deck buses with the standard type of two-door body. Number 29 was an AEC Regal with body by Brush, number 30 a Leyland Tiger TS3 and number 31 a Crossley Alpha, both bodied by Vulcan. These buses were the first in the fleet to have a service number box.

There were now 27 buses in the fleet and over 72 miles of route were being operated compared with 33 in the previous year. In the Manager's report at the time reference was made to the improvement in the financial situation. The net profit showed a total of £4,063 and the Committee decided to use some of this to meet the loss on the Radcliffe sections instead of drawing upon the Borough's rates as they were entitled to do. This still left the sum of £1,436 to be transferred to the reserve. The unfortunate conditions of trade in the area had affected the finances of the transport undertaking but the Committee was satisfied with the progress made. Improvements had been carried out by installing modern equipment, new rolling stock and the existing cars and plant had been kept in an efficient state. To do all these things and still show a profit, even though a small one at a time of acute commercial and industrial depression, was no mean achievement.

The Council congratulated the Chairman, Deputy Chairman and the Manager on the result. Apart from these circumstances, the department paid out over £60,000 in wages, its contribution to the municipal rates amounted to £2,239 and to the national exchequer £2,811. Both the Chairman and Deputy Chairman expressed their appreciation of the way in which the Manager and staff had worked to put the Tramways undertaking on a sound financial basis and there could be no doubt that their commendations were well deserved. Reference was made to the wonderful enthusiasm displayed by Mr Fenwick, the members of the administration staff, drivers, conductors and trolley boys. It was said that every one of them worked cheerfully and well. The opinion was that the Corporation had a staff that claimed the consideration and courtesy of the travelling public. The Committee were grateful that the employees took such a pride in the undertaking.

The coming of the Diesel

During 1930 the Manager reported for the information of the Tramways Committee that the Chairman and he had witnessed a demonstration of a motor fitted with a 'Diesel' engine which ran on crude oil. In September that year a diesel-engined AEC Regent demonstrator with Strachans double-deck body ran in the town for two weeks. Reaction was favourable and in June 1931 an order for five oil-engined Crossley buses was placed.

After experience of this type of engine the Department purchased twenty Leyland E151 type 8.6 litre diesel engines to replace the petrol engines in the AEC, Crossley, Daimler, Dennis and Leyland buses, the conversions taking place between 1934 and 1936. Bury Transport Department was one of the pioneers of the compression ignition (diesel) engine, being one of the first transport undertakings in the country to adopt this type of power unit. The oil engines were more economical, reducing the running costs of the buses. The price of diesel fuel was then about one third that of petrol per gallon and a diesel-engined bus could travel three times the distance of a petrol-engined bus on every gallon.

In the thirties Bury Corporation seemed unable to make up its mind on a vehicle purchasing policy, the 1931 deliveries being a prime example. These photographs show buses on three different makes of chassis, although all carry a virtually identical Brush two-door, twin staircase body.

The two upper pictures show number 28 (EN 4744), a Crossley Condor *(DBC)* and number 25 (EN 4741), a Leyland Titan TD1 *(MMT)*, standing outside the Brush Factory before delivery. Below AEC Regent number 27 (EN 4743) draws away from Black Lane station while working on service 5 from Whitefield to the Three Arrows. *(SGC)*

Despite their unorthodox bodies the Second World War assured them of a relatively long life, mostly as ARP vehicles but some, including 27 and 28, ending their days with small independents.

To cater for growing traffic demand 11 buses were added to the fleet during 1931. The first, in the February, was a former Leyland demonstrator TE 9855, a Titan TD1 model with a Leyland double-deck body. This replaced the short-lived former Lees coach and took its fleet number 24. It was unusual in the fleet, the driver having to enter the cab via the lower saloon as there was no cab door on the off-side.

In the same month the four remaining experimental buses arrived. Numbers 25 and 26 were two more Leyland Titan TD1s, number 27 was an AEC Regent and number 28 was a Crossley Condor. They all carried Brush double-deck bodies with dual doors and staircases. In August came another Condor, number 37 this time carrying a Crossley lowbridge body with two sunken gangways, one on either side of the upper deck with rows of triple seats between. Finally, in the October, came the five diesel-engined buses numbered 32-36, Crossley Condors with Crossley two-door bodies similar to the Brush bodies on numbers 25-28.

The Corporation introduced this dual-entrance design of body for its first double-deck buses and continued it on all double-deck orders until the introduction of the centre entrance buses in 1933. The conventional rear entrance and staircase were used, but in addition there was a front exit with folding doors set the length of one side window back from the bulkhead. The front staircase went up from the entrance towards the front of the bus curving to the right and emerging on the front of the upper saloon to the left of the gangway. The Brush bodies incorporated the dual-entrance feature in the exaggerated 'piano front' design favoured by this manufacturer at that time. An unusual feature on these bodies was the oval windows at the rear of the top deck and on the platform.

In April 1932 the maximum speed limit on all public service vehicles was increased to 30mph.

The Heywood saga

Mention has already been made of the 1905 agreement by which Heywood built and owned the tramways in the Borough but, instead of leasing them, allowed Bury and Rochdale to run over them while paying a proportion of the expenses and taking a share in the revenue. This effectively made it an operator in its own right and created complications for anybody operating there in the future.

By 1929 the condition of the track was beginning to cause concern and in the October protracted and often acrimonious discussions commenced on replacing the tram service between Bury and Rochdale with motorbuses. Bury and Rochdale offered to pay Heywood £9,000, which was the outstanding capital debt on the tramway within the Borough. Heywood, however, insisted that it should also be paid for reinstating the road. The view taken by Bury and Rochdale was that, as the lines were owned by Heywood and had never been leased to the operators, this cost was Heywood's responsibility.

With the Road Traffic Act on the horizon negotiations were suspended and when the Act became law Bury and Rochdale offered to run the service, take the receipts and pay the expenses. Heywood, however, faced with the cost of highway reinstatement and no income to offset it, demanded a share of the receipts similar to the arrangements which existed on the Bolton-Rochdale express service.

More talks took place but by the end of October 1931 an impasse was reached so Heywood decided it would do better operating its own buses and applied to the newly-formed Traffic Commissioners for consent to do this and also to operate a bus service of its own between Bolton, Bury, Heywood and Rochdale. Bury and Rochdale objected and finally on 13th June 1932 the Commissioners refused Heywood's application.

The three Corporations subsequently reached agreement and buses took over from trams on Sunday 3rd July 1932 when at 9.30am the first buses departed simultaneously from Bury and Rochdale. The travelling time between Bury and Heywood was 15 minutes and the same between Heywood and Rochdale. This left just a few peak hour journeys between Bury and Heywood to be operated by trams for a few months longer.

Two weeks after its introduction the Bury Times commented:

'There is a reasonableness akin to dignity about the double-deck bus. It is not one of your 'harum-scarum' types of vehicles that rush in a halo of dust and fumes, snorting and hooting along the flat roads, up the hills and down the hills, with such shaking and swaying that the passengers emerge feeling decidedly worse for wear.

No! The double-decker is of a different class - in fact a member of the aristocracy of the roads. One of the 'smart set' so to speak. He (or is it she?) is a lofty and dignified vehicle combining swiftness with smoothness, assuring you of comfort and security, and a conscientious worker all the time.

We, in Bury, are slowly but surely becoming 'double-deckerised'. The first few days of last week were full of the novelty of the thing as was quite apparent from the remarks of several of the workmen journeying on the Bury to Heywood route.

"Blooming cushy aren't they, mate?"

"Beats blinking trams, does this."

"Bit of a smell about 'em, though."

"Aye, they're oil-burners, tha' knows."

Such were the opinions passed earlier in the week. Afterwards the novelty began to pall a little. Workmen took their places in the bus with all the grace and majesty of millionaires entering their own luxurious saloons. Workmen's mode of travel has become revolutionised. We have entered an era of luxury travel at economical prices.'

To operate its share of the service Bury ordered five Daimler CP6 double-deckers with the now standard two-door body, this time by Strachan. These buses were numbered 1-5 but did not arrive until October 1932 and to introduce the service it was necessary to keep some of the very early

Leylands in operation resulting in fleet numbers 1, 3 and 4 being duplicated for a time. One of the new buses was displayed at the 1932 Motor Show at Earls Court.

Following the introduction of the new buses, Mr George Edwards, who was the Traffic Superintendent at this time, stated in an interview for the Bury Times that the town's Transport Department was doing all it could to give the best service possible for the people of Bury and District. Many years earlier Bury Tramways men had been recognised as the smartest in the country and in August 1932 new regulations had been put into force to regain this reputation. The list included the following:-

'Uniforms to be well brushed each day; buttons, badges and numbers to be polished, cash bags and ticket punch straps to be blackened and polished, white collars, black ties, black boots or shoes only to be worn. (At this time it was customary for tram and bus drivers to wear clogs as foot wear). No flowers or decorations to be worn in caps or jackets. Employees wearing shoes must wear black or blue socks; fancy light socks would not be permitted. During the summer months (1st May to 30th September) white cap covers must be worn and men must come on duty provided accordingly. The signal for wearing those covers will be the wearing of one by the inspector on 'centre' duty. When buses arrive at a terminus or town centre, drivers are to button up their coats before leaving the cab and remain

In 1932 Bury purchased another five buses on yet another chassis, this time the Daimler CP6 mated with Strachans' version of the twin-staircase body. Number 3 (EN 5292) is pictured outside the Strachans' factory. The bus lasted until 1946 when it was sold to Williams of Emsworth in Surrey, quickly passing to two other small independents before going for scrap in 1947. *(DBC)*

at the front of the bus. Conductors to remain on the bus collecting fares while the bus is standing and be ready to help aged people or children on or off and to answer politely any enquiries from intending passengers.'

The instruction further stated that

'Employees are quite aware that the public will travel by that transport which is the smartest, most courteous and obliging and it is for you to 'sell service' and to encourage people to travel by the Corporation Transport services. The safety and convenience of the travelling public must be the first consideration of every employee'.

To encourage the men in their appearances, new uniforms were issued. The jackets were double breasted with lapels and two epaulettes. On the right epaulette was a badge of the Corporation's coat of arms and the letters BCT and on the left one was the coat of arms badge and the employee's number in three digits.

Another new Manager

In October 1932 Mr Fenwick, the General Manager, wrote to the Town Clerk tendering his resignation and asking the Council to be released from his position by 21st November 1932 in order to take up an appointment as Assistant Manager of the Cape Electric Company of Cape Town, South Africa. In his letter, Mr Fenwick thanked the members of the Council and particularly the members of the Transport Committee for the kindness he had received from them. He also wished to express his appreciation of the happy relationship which had existed between the other Corporation officials and himself.

Alderman Turner, the Chairman of the Transport Committee, moved that the resignation of Mr Fenwick be accepted with regret and that the Town Clerk be instructed to place on record in the minutes the Council's appreciation of the services rendered by Mr Fenwick as Transport Manager at Bury during the past three years. Councillor Riddle, the Vice-Chairman of the Transport Committee, seconding the resolution, wished to say briefly the things which Mr Fenwick had done for the Transport undertaking. He had a splendid knowledge of the Road Traffic Act and was the equal of any Council regarding it. He had obtained all the figures and particulars which enabled the Corporation to buy Messrs Lees of

Radcliffe's undertaking at a satisfactory price and he had fixed up many satisfactory agreements with Ribble Bus Services and surrounding authorities. When the Committee had to choose a new manager three years earlier, Mr Fenwick was the youngest. The Mayor, Alderman JT Lord, remarked that Mr Fenwick's success was to the honour of Bury.

After the resignation of Mr Fenwick, the Committee advertised for a new manager. A short list of six was drawn up and on 26th January 1933 the Transport Committee interviewed the applicants and chose Cyril Percy Paige. Mr Paige was then the Traffic Manager with the West Riding Electric Tramways Company Limited and West Riding Automobile Company Limited of Castleford, Yorkshire. He was a Member of the Institute of Automobile and Electrical Engineers.

In January 1915 Mr Paige had enlisted in the Royal Flying Corps and was later in charge of engineering shops of the Royal Air Force at Lincoln and Beverley. On leaving the forces at the end of the war he was appointed Engineer to the Eastbourne Aviation Company Limited in Sussex, becoming Manager of Ashby Motor Services Limited of Tonbridge Wells in 1922. Later that year he was appointed General Manager of Bangor Blue Motors Limited in North Wales, a position he held for over seven years during which time he had great success in completely reorganising the undertaking. In 1927 he was elected an Associate Member of the Institute of Transport. At the time of his appointment at Bury he was managing a fleet of 45 double-deck buses and the previous year the tramway system had been converted to buses under his management. Mr Paige's salary when he came to Bury was £650 per year with two annual increments of £50 rising to £750.

At this time interest was growing in the provision of a 'real and permanent transport centre', in other words a bus station, in the town. A joint sub-committee of the Watch and Transport Committees discussed the matter but decided not to proceed, the main stumbling block being the cost. The question resurfaced several times over the years including a proposal to build on a concrete raft over Bolton Street station, but it was not until 1980 that Bury would get its interchange.

On 12th March, 1933 the Tramway system celebrated its Golden Jubilee (1883-1933).

Harry Orr and Sons

As mentioned earlier, the firm of H Orr and Sons Motor Bus Services of Little Lever ran bus services from Stopes to Manchester via Radcliffe and Stand Lane, from Coronation Square, Little Lever to the Coach and Horses at Breightmet, from Philips Park Road, Prestwich to Manchester and from Sedgley Park to the Tower Buildings at Prestwich. After lengthy negotiations terms were finalised in May 1933 between Bolton, Bury and Salford Corporations for the purchase of the firm. The terms were approved by Bury Council and the necessary money for the purchase was taken from the reserve fund. Finally, on Friday 23rd June 1933, at a public sitting of the North Western Traffic Commissioners, it was announced that Mr Orr would surrender his licences and the services would be taken over by the three Corporations, their buses running over the routes from the following Monday.

It was stated at the time that this was the closing of what had been a very stormy chapter. The Prestwich routes had been contested more keenly than any other in the North Western Area. Mr Orr had operated these services and seen them grow, but at this time he felt he could not refuse the terms offered him by the three Corporations, therefore, in that sense he was perfectly satisfied and expressed his appreciation of the way the Corporations had met him. 'We fought on many occasions but all that is past and gone.' said Mr Orr. 'I part with these services freely and absolutely of my own free will and quite happily.' However, it has been said elsewhere that the Traffic Commissioner forced the sale after one of Orr's buses was involved in a fatal accident when racing a tramcar.

Bury took the Stopes service with one bus from the Orr fleet. This was his TE 8365, a Leyland TD1, new in June 1929, with Leyland lowbridge bodywork and an outside staircase which in later years could usually be found on the Bolton route. On arrival at Bury it received the fleet number 38. The stairs were enclosed by Massey Brothers of Wigan during 1935 after a fatal accident.

Buses for trams

On 12th March 1933 Bury celebrated 50 years of tramway operation. Electric trams had served the town well for thirty years, but much of the tramway network had been in continuous use for a lengthy period which included the First World War when only the minimum of maintenance had taken place and the infrastructure was quite literally wearing out. Increasingly, there were complaints about the rough riding of the cars and the noise and vibration on curves and pointwork. Further, road traffic was increasing and the resulting congestion in the narrow streets in the town centre was making the trams less attractive.

At the time the well-managed and profitable tram service contributed enough income to subsidise the town's general rate. This was not unusual among tramway undertakings at the time although closer study generally shows that the main reason was insufficient allowance being made for replacement of the track and overhead at the end of its working life. This was usually because the capital equipment was written down over a longer period than the true life of the asset. In this respect Bury was neither better nor worse than many other undertakings at the time, none of which had any previous experience of running heavy tramcars at high frequencies and tended to be over optimistic. But, whatever the reasons, by the early thirties serious capital expenditure was needed and in a time of financial stringency there just wasn't enough money to carry it out.

At the meeting of the Transport Committee on 24th January 1933, as part of a discussion on the financial position of the undertaking, the Chief Administrative Assistant of the Transport Department, who was at the time acting as General Manager, put forward proposals made by Mr Fenwick for the conversion of much of the remaining system to motor bus operation. The Committee deferred any comment until the arrival of the new General Manager, but much work went on behind the scenes and at its March meeting the Committee recommended that the Town Clerk should apply to the Ministry of Transport for permission to abandon tramcar services on the routes from Bury to Heywood, Breightmet, Tottington, Jericho and Walmersley and from Dumers Lane to Whitefield, the dates of abandonment of each section to be decided by the Committee. This was in effect all the remaining tramways except for the cars still operating at peak times on the Radcliffe routes to comply with the Radcliffe agreements.

The Town Clerk was instructed to inform the other local authorities concerned and ten additional fuel oil buses were purchased to replace the trams on the first section to be changed over. These turned out to be AEC Regents, two (39/40) bodied by Northern Counties and eight (41-48) by Roe to the current two-door design which arrived between October and December 1933. They had AEC 8.8 litre diesel engines, Daimler pre-selector gearboxes with pedestal selection and fluid flywheel transmission.

The remaining peak period tram journeys between Bury and Heywood came off almost immediately and were replaced by motor buses on service 14 from 19th February 1933 and at the same time Bury ceased to run on service 18 between Heywood and Manchester, Manchester Corporation taking over the working. Next to go was the Manchester Road route on 16th October 1933 when the Bury to Whitefield section was replaced by bus service 7, thus ending joint operation with Salford on service 63 to Manchester and leaving only the Bury to Dumers Lane portion used by the Radcliffe cars.

It had been intended that the tram service between Bury and Bolton would have been the first to end on 3rd September and that buses would operate the service from the following day, but it was not until 4th December that the Council heard that the Traffic Commissioners had granted the necessary licences. The Committee's original idea was to run the service through between Bolton and Rochdale but in the event this did not happen.

At 10.45pm on the night of Sunday 21st January 1934 the last tram ran from Bury to Bolton. The Bury Times reported:-

'It was drizzling with rain in the Market Place as the driver released the brake and set the tram in motion on the last journey to Bolton. There was no one to wave it on its way. How different was this brooding atmosphere as the tram left, from that which prevailed on 6th May 1907 when the whole town turned out to welcome the first Bolton to Bury car. That first car was bedecked gaily and people spoke of the electric car as having come to stay. It was a time of jubilation. But on Sunday there was not a cheer as the tram left for Bolton. Our age has grown sophisticated and the piecemeal, sectional substitution of petrol-driven buses for tramcars does not seem to justify celebrations. Perhaps in another thirty years we shall marvel at transport development and hail some new mechanical conveyance that will travel at incredible speed.'

The following morning, Monday 22nd January, the Bury to Bolton service was run by double-deck buses numbered 23T, the T standing for tram to distinguish the journeys from those on the former express service which showed 23. The travelling time on the round journey was reduced by ten minutes. At the Bolton end, the trams had only gone as far as Bradshawgate, but the buses went over Trinity Street Station bridge to Newport Street and Great Moor Street where the terminus was, returning to Bury via Bradshawgate and Bridgeman Place.

After these conversions a number of redundant tramcars were stored in the depot so the Transport Committee instructed the Manager to arrange for the dismantling of a number of old trams and to sell the materials. It was mentioned that with the combination of carpentry skill and the ingenuity of decorating art, the bodies of old trams could be converted into respectable looking sports pavilions, and with a greater degree of camouflage they might even pass as modern sun houses. According to the 'Bury Times' some people who came into possession of tram bodies had them transported to country places and with one or two additions, a quantity of light furniture, a portable cooker and heating appliances plus a few yards of curtain material had transformed them into week-end bungalows which were at once serviceable and economical.

Use of these obsolete bodies as waiting rooms for bus companies at their depots was not uncommon. Two of Bury's old tram bodies were put in Hoyle's playing fields and used as shelters and another was put in Rochdale Road recreation ground for the tennis section's use as a pavilion. At the depot, two ends of top decks were used as foreman's offices, one in the body shop and the other in the paint shop, the former being dismantled and disposed of in July 1975. The one in the paint shop was still in use for this purpose until the depot was closed in July 1985 when it was taken to the Greater Manchester Museum of Transport at Boyle Street, Cheetham. There it was cleaned up and put on display and during the cleaning process was found to have been part of car number 7. A few of these tram bodies were purchased for use as summerhouses and sheds, one being at Heywood Old Road, Simister where it was re-discovered in 1983 and is now in the Museum of Science and Industry at Liverpool Road Station, Manchester.

Only two buses entered service in 1934, both of which arrived in the August and were purchased for evaluation as forerunners of larger orders for the planned tramway conversions. Number 49 was a Crossley Mancunian of the type which had replaced the Condor while number 50 was a Leyland Titan TD3c with torque converter transmission. Both carried a new design of body by English Electric incorporating a centre entrance and twin staircases. These and all subsequent buses had diesel engines.

The torque converter provided a fully automatic transmission apart from a manually engaged direct drive that was the equivalent of top gear. It was controlled by a selector lever which replaced the normal gear lever and had four positions; converter, direct, neutral and reverse. There was no clutch pedal. The converter was used for all conditions from stationary up to top gear speeds when the direct drive was selected. The torque converter did away with gear changing and some operators like Bury took large numbers of these vehicles for tramway conversions considering it easier to train former tram drivers on them rather than on conventional buses with a clutch and crash gearbox.

The next route to be considered for conversion was that to Jericho, Bury's first electric tram route dating back to 1903. Leyland TT2 Titanics from a batch of five numbered 51-55 took over the new service 9 on 2nd January 1935. These six-wheel vehicles carried an English Electric centre entrance double-deck body seating 60 passengers which was ideal for clearing the queues on this short, heavily loaded service.

In the week of 6th May 1935, to celebrate the Silver Jubilee of King George V and Queen Mary, the Corporation opened the depot to the public. Visitors were given a conducted tour with explanations as to the uses and reasons of equipment with some demonstrations showing how they worked and craftsmen could be seen carrying out their tasks.

In February 1936 a request was received from the residents in the Baldingstone area asking the Committee to provide a bus service between Bury and Nangreaves, a small hamlet on the moors beyond Walmersley. The Committee turned down the request, but was at pains to point out that it had not done so without serious consideration. The route had been surveyed very carefully and it had been found very dangerous for two vehicles to pass along at the same time, and that there was no turning place. The matter rumbled on but it would be a number of years before road improvements and housing development made it possible for the route to be introduced.

Experience with torque converter-fitted Leyland TD3 number 50 in 1934 had evidently been satisfactory, as seven more, this time newer TD4 models, were ordered with Leyland's own double-deck body with a conventional rear platform which was to become Bury's standard for a number of years. Arriving in June 1936 they carried fleet numbers 56-62.

Four more identical examples arrived in March 1937 as replacements for withdrawn older buses and took vacant numbers 31, 34, 35 and 37.

Later in 1937 one of Bury's double deck buses, Leyland TD3 number 50, was sent to the local firm of HE Aspin of Daisyfield, Bury for experiments with a new type of rotary valve engine. Although it spent many weeks at Aspins it is believed that no Aspin engine was ever fitted to it. At that time the company was experimenting with this type of engine that ticked over at 2,000rpm. It was felt that an engine revolving at that speed would have been dangerous with a conventional clutch so number 50 was used as it had a torque converter transmission. A motorcycle and a racing car were also used in these experiments.

Trouble in Radcliffe

The existing agreement with Radcliffe which obliged Bury to run trams in the Borough expired in June 1935, although at Radcliffe's request buses had operated the majority of the service for the last five years with only a minimal tram presence at peak periods to keep within the terms of the agreement. So negotiations were started with Radcliffe Council and by 12th December 1934 a new agreement was drawn up whereby Bury would take all the revenue and pay all the expenses, the resulting profit or loss to be shared between the two undertakings on a mileage basis. This new agreement was to last for 15 years and would be overseen by a joint Management Sub-

Pictured upper left parked behind the old Market Hall is number 47 (EN 5640), a 1933 AEC Regent with a somewhat austere Roe body. Despite their old-fashioned appearance these were sturdy vehicles and number 47 lasted until 1950 becoming a showman's caravan. *(SGC)*

Lower left is number 52 (EN 6051), one of the five massive Leyland Titanics bought for the conversion of the Jericho service in 1935. It lasted through the war being withdrawn in 1946 and was one of a pair which went to Derby Corporation Building Department. *(DBC)*

Below is number 58 (EN 6714), one of seven Leyland TD4cs which comprised the 1936 deliveries. It is fitted with a Leyland 48-seat body, although a further four seats were added soon after its arrival. It was withdrawn in 1948 and sold for scrap. *(DBC)*

Committee consisting of four representatives from each authority, its recommendations to be subject to ratification by the Transport Committees of both Bury and Radcliffe.

That portion of the Bury to Bolton service in the Radcliffe area along Bolton Road was excluded from the agreement but for a three month trial period Bury agreed to operate a service between Radcliffe town centre and Ainsworth, which had just been incorporated in Radcliffe Borough, on a cost/revenue sharing basis between the two undertakings. If demand for the service was not found to be satisfactory it could be continued at Radcliffe's expense, or if satisfactory it would be included in the agreement.

This was all very nice and gentlemanly, but Radcliffe had just become a Municipal Borough and was flexing its muscles. Whether by accident or design it never ratified the agreement; Bury ran the service to Ainsworth for three months but it lacked the necessary support and it was withdrawn at the end of the trial period. Radcliffe was none too happy with this and relations were strained for some time. Then Bury proposed to lift the track on Manchester Road and Dumers Lane as part of its programme to convert the remainder of its system to buses.

Radcliffe, of course, found the situation unacceptable and on 19th July 1937 wrote to Bury stating that it proposed to run its own tramway service and for that purpose asked Bury to sell them the trams currently employed in operating the services within Radcliffe and also for consent to operate through services to Bury town centre. The Transport Committee considered this carefully and agreed to sell some cars to Radcliffe, but that the request to be allowed to run through services to Bury town centre be refused as it would mean leaving the track in place in Bury.

With this difference of opinion between the two councils, the Traffic Commissioners held an Inquiry into Bury Corporation's application for licences in Manchester Town Hall on 9th September 1937 under the Chairmanship of Mr William Chamberlain. Radcliffe's objections were over the wording of the agreement, the withdrawal of the trams and their replacement by buses and its request for a service between Radcliffe and Ainsworth. Radcliffe also wanted the trams to run through from the Three Arrows to Whitefield but again this was not possible as Salford Corporation

had, in March of that year, removed the track and overhead equipment between Whitefield Railway Station and the borough boundary at Goats Gate.

The Traffic Commissioner reserved his decision and instructed that Radcliffe's representatives should meet with their opposite numbers from Bolton, Bury and Salford Transport Departments and Lancashire United Transport to look at services in the Radcliffe area generally and sort things out between them. On 11th October 1937 the managers of the four municipal undertakings met at Bury Town Hall to prepare a scheme on the lines suggested by the Traffic Commissioner, the proposals being approved in July 1938.

On 9th October 1938 the last trams ran in Radcliffe and the following day bus services were revised to provide improved links across the district. Alternate journeys on Bury service 16 (Bury-Radcliffe-Stopes) were extended through Little Lever and Moses Gate to Bolton as service 52 jointly operated by Bury and Bolton Corporations and Salford service 24 between Victoria Bus Station and Whitefield was extended to Radcliffe via Ringley Road and Stand Lane.

Service 5 between Whitefield and the Three Arrows via Radcliffe New Road was revised comprehensively. Some journeys were extended to Ainsworth and short workings between Whitefield and Radcliffe were renumbered 15 with some journeys diverted via Ringley Road and Stand Lane numbered 20.

The track was then lifted in Dumers Lane and along Manchester Road to Starkies, the short section from there to Bury town centre being left intact for services to the Bury FC ground at Gigg Lane on match days.

The gathering storm

The last few years of the decade were a troubled time as the world drifted slowly but inexorably towards war. But after the trauma of the abdication of King Edward VIII the Coronation of his younger brother the Duke of York as King George VI on 12th May 1937 was a bright spark in the gloom. To commemorate the event the Corporation opened the tram and bus depot to the public and invited them to come and inspect it during Monday, Tuesday, Thursday, Friday and Saturday of Coronation week, 10th to 15th May 1937. Conducted tours of the depot took place at 2pm,

During 1937 lengthy negotiations were taking place between Bury and Radcliffe Corporations in regard to the future of the tramways in Radcliffe. These were to drag on until well into 1938 before agreement was finally reached on the withdrawal of the trams and the introduction of a new network of bus services in their place. Meanwhile, the trams kept running. In the upper view a cyclist stops for a rest at the top of Ainsworth Road at the Three Arrows while tram number 15 is about to leave on an evening peak working and a Bury Corporation Leyland passes on the service journey. Below, tram number 11 tops the incline and crosses the railway line at Knowsley Street station on its way into Bury from Radcliffe. *(Both DBC)*

Number 34 (EN 6972) was another Leyland TD4c with Leyland body, one of four delivered in 1937. It was renumbered to 82 in 1945 and is pictured upper right standing on Knowsley Street after its morning peak duty. It was withdrawn in 1950 and, along with a number of other Bury buses, passed to Paton of Renfrew where it ran for another eight years. *(SGC)*

In the middle view Leyland TD5c number 67 (EN 7295), also with Leyland body, stands in Moss Street with Kay Gardens and Haymarket Street in the background before leaving on service 21 to Rochdale. It was withdrawn in 1952 and passed to Lansdowne Luxury Coaches in London. *(DBC)*

Below, number 76 (EN 8113) was one of the last buses delivered to Bury before the beginning of the war. It was a Leyland TD5 with bodywork by Northern Counties and is pictured in Moss Street before leaving for Bullfinch Drive. *(SGC)*

4pm and 7pm which took in 26 separate points of interest where the visitors could see work being carried out in routine inspections, replacements and general everyday running and maintenance at the depot. A brochure was published in which the Mayor set out a brief history of the Department whre he mentioned that in 1925 the Corporation commenced the operation of buses which proved so popular as to eventually replace the trams on a number of routes. In their day the trams had proved to be a good proposition for the town. He said the Transport Department was constantly seeking methods to improve its usefulness and priority was given to supply a safe and efficient service, rather than making large profits. He appealed to the public to make the maximum use of and to patronise the services provided.

Councillor Riddle, the Chairman of the Transport Committee, added a few words. He hoped that many members of the public would take advantage of the opportunity to visit the works because he felt that very few people had any real idea of the amount of organisation needed to supply the public with a safe and satisfactory service. During the previous few years considerable re-organisation had taken place in the Department. It was stated that at that time the Department had 95 passenger vehicles comprising 33 tramcars and 62 buses and many of the buses had been fitted with diesel engines. Councillor Riddle noted that during 1936 these 95 vehicles had carried 23,622,727 passengers.

Thirteen buses were delivered in 1938. First, in January came nine Leyland TD5c Titans with standard Leyland 52-seat double-deck bodies numbered 63-71, followed in October by four Leyland TS8c Tigers with 36-seat front-entrance single-deck bodies by Burlingham, taking the numbers 72-75. Once again, they all had torque converters.

Five more Leyland TD5s came in July 1939, this time with the standard crash gearbox. These had 56-seat rear-entrance bodies built by Northern Counties of Wigan at a cost of £1,667 10s 0d per vehicle and were numbered 76-80.

As time rolled on the political situation in Europe worsened and preparations were made for the now inevitable outbreak of war with Germany. Air raid shelters were erected, staff were given training on how to deal with unexploded bombs and blackout exercises were carried out. The urgent preparation for hostilities with Germany was affecting the production and supply of all kinds of equipment and the following extract from a tender by AEC Ltd sums up the situation.

'Unfortunately, the very heavy rearmament programme is severely taxing the demands for essential materials absorbed in commercial enterprise, and although we have every reason to believe that the deliveries aforementioned can be achieved, we are unable to accept a penalty restriction for any delay, and would respectfully ask for this to be excluded from the terms of the contract.'

On 1st September 1939 German tanks rolled into Poland and two days later Britain declared war on Germany. The Second World War had begun.

At the outbreak of war the following services were being run:

Tram	Walmersley-Bury-Tottington
1	Bury-Walshaw
2	Bury-Ainsworth
3	Bury-Ramsbottom-Rawtenstall
4	Bury-Edenfield-Rawtenstall
5	Whitefield-Ainsworth
6	*Bury-Radcliffe via Dumers Lane (16)*
7	Bury-Whitefield
8	Blackford Bridge-Whitefield
9	Bury-Jericho
10	*Bury-Wham Bar (21)*
11	*Bury-Heap Bridge (21)*
12	*Bury-Starling (2)*
14	*Bury-Heywood (21)*
15	*Whitefield-Radcliffe (5)*
16	Bury-Stopes via Dumers Lane
18	*Bury-Top o' th' Cross (16)*
19	Bury-Rochdale via Jericho
20	Whitefield-Radcliffe via Stand Lane
21	Bury-Heywood-Rochdale
22	*Bury-Jolly Carters (23T)*
23T	Bury-Bolton
24	*Bury-Three Arrows (23T)*
25	Bury-Farnworth via Warth
26	*Bury-Breightmet (23T)*
27	*Bury-New Bridge (16)*
35	Bury-Manchester

Services in italics were peak hour short workings, the all day service being shown in brackets.

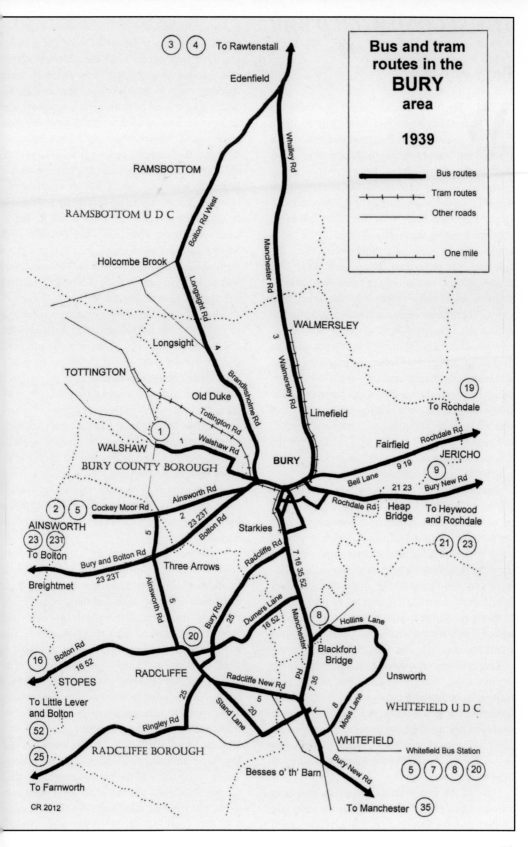

Bus and tram routes in the **BURY** area

1939

Bus routes
Tram routes
Other roads

One mile

THE SECOND WORLD WAR

Bury at war

When the war started the first thing the Department had to do was to make sure that all the trams and buses were blacked out at night so that they showed no lights that would be visible to enemy aircraft flying overhead. Shields were fitted over the headlights to cut down the amount of light emitted and also stopped the light being seen from above. Narrow slits were put in these shields so that the lights could only be seen at ground level. Even the side and rear lights had covers over them. The mudguards and corners of the buses were painted white to make them more visible to other road users. The interior lights were also modified to reduce the amount of light showing outside and this was done either by using lower wattage bulbs or putting covers over them. To make the trams and buses safe from glass being shattered through bomb blast and showering on the passengers, the windows were covered with a cotton mesh that was stuck on to the glass with shellac. A small hole about 2 inches in diameter was cut in the centre of the mesh to allow passengers to see where they were during daylight.

Passengers waiting at stops were advised to signal drivers to stop by waving a newspaper or a white handkerchief and conductors were instructed to call out the name of each stop as at night it would have been almost impossible for passengers to know where they were unless they were very familiar with the route. Later, battery lamps were issued to conductors to be attached to their cash bag strap so that they could see what money they were tendered, what ticket they issued from their clip rack, and what change they gave.

One problem encountered on the trams during the black-out was re-locating the trolley pole back into contact with the overhead wires at each terminus. As it was dark the conductors were unable to see the wire, so this was done by a hit and miss method, waiting to feel the arm touch the wire and watching for the sparks as the trolley head touched it.

One of the first wartime economy measures introduced by the Government was the rationing of fuel and the Department quickly introduced a drastically reduced service on both trams and buses amounting to about 42% of the mileage. On 17th September 1939 the Burnley service was handed over to Ribble with Bury buses working only to Ramsbottom, Rawtenstall and Water. At the same time the service numbers were transposed, 3 being used for the Walmersley Road route and 4 for journeys via Ramsbottom. On the same day services in Radcliffe were revised, the Bury-Farnworth service (25) was cut back to Radcliffe with the Radcliffe-Farnworth section being worked as a separate service by LUT and 2, Rochdale-Bolton and 52 Bury-Radcliffe-Bolton were withdrawn. Then, on 22nd October 1939 Salford cut its 24 service back to Whitefield and on 4th December the Radcliffe to Whitefield route was diverted in part to run via Stand Lane, these journeys being renumbered 20.

Most of the other services suffered reduction in frequency but in the case of 21 between Bury and Rochdale the two operators could not agree and the service was split at Heywood from 25th September, both halves running on different frequencies although eventually common sense prevailed and buses ran through again.

The tram line between Market Street and Gigg Lane, Starkies, used only for football specials was re-opened for a part-day service to relieve the buses on this short stretch at peak periods. It was usually operated by the two remaining 4-wheel cars; number 30, the car rebuilt for the short-lived Manchester service and number 38. Later it ran on Saturdays only.

A number of men from the Department were enlisted into the Army, Navy and Air Force in all about 130 men from the road staff, depot and office going to fight for their country. The positions that were left vacant by these men were first offered to their relatives and to take some of their places women were recruited to work as cleaners, clerks or conductresses. This was the second time that conductresses had been employed, both due to wartime conditions. Some of the men who remained were trained to drive the trams and buses. The wives of the men who went into the forces were paid their husband's wage less their military pay, the Corporation doing this in recognition of the men's devotion to their country. Not only did the staff cover their own work, but most of them were involved in some way with Civil Defence, Fire Watching, Air-raid

The last of Bury's pre-war orders arrived between June and August 1940. These were nine Leyland Titan TD7s, five bodied by Northern Counties and four by Weymann. Originally allocated numbers 81-89, they were immediately renumbered to 16-19 and 6-10 respectively but may not even have carried their original allotted numbers. In 1946 they were again renumbered 85-93. Northern Counties-bodied number 81 (EN 8249) is shown above standing in Knowsley Street about 1950 displaying its final number 85. It was withdrawn and scrapped in 1953. *(SGC)* Pictured below before leaving the Weymann factory is number 88 (EN 8247). Withdrawn in 1952 it passed via a London dealer to Lansdowne Luxury Coaches of Leytonstone. *(MMT)*

Wardens, or Special Constabulary. Although Bury was not seriously affected by air-raid damage, countless hours were spent on stand-by duties. Destination boxes on the buses and trams were painted out as an invasion precaution and also to hinder any German airman who may have had his aircraft shot down and had parachuted to safety and was trying to find his bearings. What he would have made of 'Jericho' is anybody's guess. Destinations were, however, restored after a short period.

At the beginning of the war nine of the Department's older buses, Leyland Lions 6-11 and Dennises 16-18 were taken over by the War Department and converted to ambulances or water carriers and were held in store ready for emergency use during enemy raids. However, there is no evidence that they were ever used for anything more than practice.

Two routes were still being operated by trams; the Walmersley and Tottington services which were run as a through service across the town centre. These had been scheduled for early withdrawal but to conserve fuel the Transport Committee decided to keep the trams running. The lack of petrol for private cars and motor cycles gave the public little choice but to travel by public transport and this put more passengers on the reduced number of buses and trams. Nine Leyland TD7s arrived between June and August 1940, 81-85 bodied by Weymann and 86-89 by Northern Counties. All had rear entrances with 56 seats. Within a few months these buses were renumbered, 81-85 becoming 6-10 and 86-89 becoming 16-19 although there was never any explanation why this should have been necessary.

During January 1941 tram number 16 was decorated with the silhouette of a battleship to advertise "War Weapons Week" and a year later this same silhouette was used on a tram (probably the same one) to advertise the "Warships Week" in the town.

A familiar poster, seen around the town and the country nationally at the time, asked everyone the question; 'Is your journey really necessary?'

After the bombing blitz of Coventry in late 1940 a request for buses and crews was sent out to bus operators throughout the country. Bury was unable to send any buses but two drivers, Tommy Minchall and Harry Schofield, volunteered to go and spent quite a few months driving buses for Midland Red in and around the bombed city. To add a little romantic sequel to this story, Tommy Minchall met a conductress, Miss Ethel Ayme from Ashby-de-la-Zouch, who was also on loan. Later they were married and came to live in Bury where they worked together as driver and conductress for many years until they both retired in the early 1960s.

In view of the call up of men for the armed forces, the Ministry of War Transport had intimated in September 1941 that the Regional Transport Commissioners were prepared to grant permits to women qualified to act as drivers of single deck buses. The Committee agreed to train and employ women in this capacity when the necessity arose but, as far as is known, no women were trained or employed for this work at Bury at that time. The Board of Trade also instructed the Department in November 1941 that employees must surrender clothing coupons when they were supplied with new uniform clothing.

The darkest hour

The loss of Burma and Malaya to the Japanese in 1942 cut off supplies of rubber and led to a further tightening of belts. By April 1942 the supply of vermilion paint was becoming difficult to obtain so it was agreed that grey paint should be used and several buses were painted all over grey. Other materials were also in short supply and, with the lack of spares and men to do the work, the tram track, especially at crossovers, became badly worn. Bus parts also became very hard to come by and some buses were cannibalised to keep others on the road. Some were even fitted with wooden slatted seats.

With the continuing shortage of fuel the Government instructed all operators with over 100 vehicles to convert 10% of their fleet to use Producer Gas instead of petrol or diesel fuel. The coke-fired gas plant produced fumes which, when mixed with water vapour, formed a gas which could then be mixed with fuel in the cylinders .At that time Bury had only 79 buses and so it was not compulsory, but the Council thought it was a good idea and decided to obtain a gas producer plant for experimental purposes. What happened with this plant, if it ever was obtained, is not known although the Department did experiment with a motor-cycle powered by gas manufactured at the local gas works but nothing further is known about it. In the event none of Bury's buses was powered by gas unlike some other towns and cities.

During the war buses were used for transporting soldiers and prisoners of war. Soldiers were taken each day by bus from Wellington Barracks on Bolton Road to Barton Docks on the Manchester Ship Canal. A prisoner of war camp was situated on Radcliffe Road near Warth Bridge where mainly Italian prisoners were held. These men were transported from the railway stations to the camp on Bury buses, mainly at night.

Alderman J Whitehead, the Chairman of the Transport Committee, and Councillor J Duckworth, the Chairman of the Cleansing Committee, appealed to the public to help in salvaging used tram and bus tickets. Alderman Whitehead referred to the wastage through the untidy habit of depositing used tickets on the roadway. 'These tickets are valuable scrap', he said, 'And it is in the national interest to salvage all we can. Every effort is made by the Transport Department to collect them from the used ticket boxes.' Councillor Duckworth added that they were anxious to reclaim all possible waste paper and with the help of the public much labour could be saved for important war work. These used tickets were collected, put in sacks and sent for recycling.

During March 1942 the Regional Transport Commissioners made an order that stopping places for public service vehicles should be arranged on the basis of four to the mile in order to save fuel and prolong the life of the vehicles and asked for the elimination of those stops that could be abandoned without creating unreasonable inconvenience to the travelling public and a Sub-Committee was appointed to look into the matter and liaise with the Commissioners. This resulted in the elimination of 26 bus stops and the resiting of eight others in the whole of the Bury and Radcliffe area. As a further measure of economy stopping places on the tram routes were reviewed to decide which ones could be withdrawn from use. The Sub-Committee inspected the Walmersley to Tottington route on Sunday 3rd May 1942, following which it recommended that 13 stops should be deleted and adjustments made to another eight.

The Council received many requests to have the withdrawn stops reinstated but refused on the grounds that the country's economy was more important. A decision was also made at the time that the last journeys from the town centre would be about 10pm. After the war and when fuel rationing was abolished only a few of the deleted bus stops were reinstated.

From time to time the Regional Transport Commissioners visited the Department to make suggestions about the services and the running of the depot. The Ministry of Works too had a say in the working of the Department. The Transport Committee was instructed to allow the Ministry to acquire the ornamental bases on the tramway standards to be melted down due to the urgent need for steel.

Early in 1943 three of the newest bogie cars, numbers 55, 56 and 58, were sold to Bolton Corporation becoming its 451 to 453 respectively, 55 and 56 operating in Bury livery with Bury fleet numbers for some time before being repainted in Bolton colours. Number 451 later received a pair of bogies from a scrapped Bolton car. One of the original 4-wheel cars, number 21, was also sold to Bolton receiving the number 331 in that fleet.

By now new bus production was limited to Daimler and Guy and they were allocated under the Acquisition and Disposal of Motor Vehicles Order 1941, on permits issued by the Regional Traffic Commissioner, operators having no choice in what they got. Bury received three buses in 1943 numbered 11, 28 and 33, filling gaps vacated by withdrawn buses. All had utility bodies by Massey on Daimler CWA6 chassis. These were basic but sturdy work horses and lasted until 1959. They had wooden slat seats. The bodies were modernised and fitted with upholstered seats in 1947 and all three were re-bodied by Roe in 1951. After withdrawal by Bury in 1959 they saw further service with small independents for a number of years.

On 29th January 1944 the Transport Manager, Mr Paige, tendered his resignation following his appointment as General Manager and Engineer of Oldham Corporation Transport Department. Alderman Whitehead, the Chairman of the Transport Committee, put on record the Committee's high appreciation of the services rendered by Mr Paige as Transport Manager during the past eleven years and their good wishes for his success and prosperity for the future. The Town Clerk was instructed to advertise for

Tram 55 was one of three cars sold to Bolton Corporation in 1943. Carrying its Bolton number 451 it is seen above in 1945 on the Chorley Old Road service. *(STA)*

Below a passenger hurries to board tram number 5, complete with its headlight shield, as it stands outside the Parish Church on its way to Tottington. *(ADP)*

Bury only received three wartime utility buses, all of which had a varied life with the Corporation. They were Daimler CWA6 chassis delivered in 1943 and carried Massey's spartan utility body with slatted wood seats taking the vacant numbers 11, 28 and 33.

In the upper view number 33 (EN 8414), by then renumbered 96, was a picture of neglect when photographed during 1947 still in its original wartime grey livery. *(DBC)*

That year the trio were refurbished with upholstered seats, more opening windows and painted in the new apple green livery. Now 94, number 11 (EN 8407) is pictured at the same spot and it seems likely that the two photographs were taken together to show the before and after condition. *(DBC)*

In 1952 all three received new Roe bodies and number 28 (EN 8408), now 95, is pictured in this form below. *(SGC)* All were withdrawn in 1959 and saw further service with other operators.

applicants for the position of Manager at a salary of £750 a year, rising by three annual increments of £50 to a maximum of £900 a year.

A short list of six applicants was invited to attend for interview on 22nd March 1944 and from this the Committee selected Mr Richard LeFevre. Due to the war regulations regarding manpower, his appointment was subject to the consent of the District Manpower Board and the Ministry of Labour and National Service but the Board and the Ministry had no objection to this appointment although the Town Clerk had to make an application for Mr LeFevre's deferment from the forces.

Mr LeFevre commenced his service with Bury Corporation on 1st May 1944. A native of Kent and a Graduate of London University, he had started his training with the Bexley Urban District Council Tramways and Electrical Undertaking. This was followed by a two year period at Plymouth where he was appointed Assistant Engineer on the completion of his training in 1925. He moved to Leigh Corporation in 1939. At the time of his appointment at Bury Mr LeFevre was 40 years of age and was a member of the Institute of Mechanical Engineers and of the Institute of Transport.

In February 1944 Bury agreed to contribute towards the cost of enlarging the bus station at Whitefield where, up to that time, buses had had to reverse on to the boarding points. The Committee instructed the Manager to negotiate with Salford Corporation and Whitefield Urban District Council on the basis of an annual payment at a rate proportionate to the use of Bury's buses. This agreement was reached with the payment based on the percentage of each authority using the station.

The return of peace

The German retreat on all fronts culminating in the D-Day landings in France in June 1944 reversed the fortunes of the war. The Allies were now winning and a new spirit of optimism was apparent.

At a Transport Committee meeting on 19th June 1944 it was decided to change the colour scheme of the bus fleet. Most of the operators around Manchester were using a red livery for their vehicles, albeit of different shades, so it was considered that Bury's should be different. The livery chosen was apple green with deep primrose around the windows and dark green mudguards, which would be applied as buses became due for repainting. The first bus to be painted in the new colours was number 70, a 1938 Leyland TD5c which had received a new grey-painted Northern Counties body in 1943 after its original Leyland body was damaged by fire in the depot. It re-entered service later in June 1944. The crews christened the buses the 'Green Linnets'. Apart from two which were painted grey, the trams retained their slowly fading red and cream livery to the end as it was not considered worth spending any money on them.

In September 1944, with the end of enemy air raids, blackout restrictions were eased on the main roads and in the town centre and in the November the Regional Traffic Commissioner allowed last buses to leave at their pre-war times. On 9th May 1945 the war ended in Europe. Overnight the masks over the headlights and saloon lighting were removed, the white patches on the mudguards and rear corners were quickly painted out and a semblance of normality returned.

Of the men who had gone to war from the Transport Department, eight had been killed in action and three were decorated for their gallantry, comprising one Order of the British Empire (OBE), one Distinguished Flying Medal (DFM) and one Military Medal (MM). Just after the war it was a common occurrence to see drivers and conductors wearing their service uniforms whilst working on the buses. Air Force blue and Army khaki were a familiar sight but this lasted only a short time until the Department could obtain a new issue of uniform clothing.

The Nations Victory Parade was held in London on 8th June 1946. Among those chosen to represent the Road Passenger Transport Industry in this parade was Bury tram driver Mr Harvey Fitton, who had worked with the Corporation for thirty-seven years as a conductor and later as a tram driver.

After working for six years the last six conductresses left the undertaking in September 1946. They had been taken on by the Department in place of men enlisted into the forces during the war. The Corporation gave these ladies, who also included some women bus cleaners who worked at the depot, a 'Thank You' dinner at the Athenaeum on 7th October 1946. There were 120 former conductresses and women cleaners at the dinner and Mr LeFevre said, "Up to the outbreak of the war the Department was held in high esteem and there is no doubt that you girls maintained that high standard. You had blackout difficulties, overloading difficulties and curtailed mileage, but you carried on cheerfully. The Committee is very grateful for what you did." They were joined by their husbands and friends later in the evening at a dance in the Derby Hall when each of the ladies was given an illuminated certificate acknowledging their work for the Department during the war years.

Six months later the Department was sending out letters requesting these same ladies to return to the buses as not enough men were taking up their old positions and the Department was short of conductors.

The war is over and No 10 rests outside the Parish Church ready to leave for Tottington. Number 10 was one of the first batch of cars dating from 1903 and, heavily rebuilt, would be one of the last to be withdrawn 46 years later in 1949. *(MMT)*

STARTING AGAIN

Hard times

Euphoria at the coming of peace did not last long. The war was still going on in the Far East and there were shortages and rationing at home, so things did not change very much in practical terms for the average Bury resident. There was a need to concentrate scarce resources on rebuilding the damaged or worn-out infrastructure: there were arrears of maintenance and spare parts and many of the Department's employees were still away in the armed forces. Perversely, after years of restrictions, demand for travel was booming.

The Ministry of Transport stopped issuing licences for the purchase and disposal of vehicles from 1st January 1946. Now every operator wanted new buses to replace worn out vehicles and to increase their fleets to cater for the explosion in demand, but the Government's 'Export or die' policy was that exports must come first to pay off the huge war debt.

After a struggle lasting several years, bus manufacturers and public transport operators had at last persuaded the Ministry of Transport to increase the maximum permitted width of buses from 7ft 6ins to 8ft providing that they kept to approved roads, the new regulations coming into effect from February 1946. The manufacturers contended that this belated concession would enable them to compete on better terms for the export trade while the operators claimed that they would be able to give the public a measure of comfort long overdue and facilitate the work of conductors in collecting fares in crowded vehicles.

After the war Bury's bus fleet was, like those of a lot of other towns, in urgent need of repair and replacement, only twelve new buses having been delivered during the war years. Unfortunately, demand was outstripping the ability to serve it; there was still fuel rationing, spares for the trams and buses were still in short supply and the population was increasing with the soldiers, sailors and airmen returning to civilian life. Complaints of inadequate services were coming from all parts of the town and requests were being received by the Council for more frequent services and new bus routes to be introduced. Petitions signed by residents were put before the Transport Committee, each area claiming it had a genuine case for more buses to be put on its route. The first new service to be introduced, on 18th March 1946, was to Ferngrove, a small housing estate to the north of Rochdale Old Road known as the 'Dicky Bird' due to the names of its roads. It was reached by a circuitous route along Market Street, Wellington Road, Heywood Street, Bond Street and Parsonage Street thus also giving the residents of the Heywood Street area the service they had sought for so many years. The new service 29 terminated at Bullfinch Drive, at the far end of the estate which would later be cut in two by the new M66 Motorway.

Then the following year, on 19th February 1947, service 28 commenced serving housing at the bottom of Alfred Street south of Parkhills Road.

A minor renumbering took place in 1946. Leyland TD4s 31, 34, 35 and 37 became 81-84, Leyland TD7s 6-10 and 16-19 became 85-93 and Daimler CWA6s 11, 28 and 33 became 94-96.

To give some indication of Bury's shortage of buses, no fewer than 52 new vehicles were ordered in 1945, the first 20 arriving between March and July 1946. Five were Crossley's new DD42/3 model, developed from the prototype which had been operating in Manchester for two years. Fitted with Crossley's own double-deck body to the Manchester design, they were numbered 97-101. The other 15 were Leyland PD1 Titans with bodies by Roe, numbered 102-116.

The remaining 32 buses came between December 1946 and August 1947 and comprised 13 more Leyland PD1s and PD1As with bodies by Northern Counties numbered 117-129, four Leyland PS1 Tigers with Roe single-deck bodies numbered 130-133 and a final 15 PD1As numbered 134-148, this time with bodies by Weymann. Once these were delivered there were only 12 buses in the fleet more than ten years old. Some of the buses had been ordered for tramway replacement but this was not to happen just yet and meanwhile Bury unexpectedly found itself with a temporary surplus and so was able to lend a number of older buses to other undertakings. Two Leyland Lions 14 and 15 dating back to 1930 were loaned to St Helens Corporation and other ageing vehicles went to Rochdale, Sheffield and Southport for a time.

Bury's first post war orders comprised twenty buses which arrived in 1946. Numerically the first five were Crossley DD42/3 models, carrying Crossley 56-seat bodies to Manchester's design with a low bonnet, deep cab windows and two smaller windows to the rear of the body side. Number 97 (EN 8531) is pictured above in Moss Street soon after delivery. It was withdrawn with the rest of the batch in 1958 and lay derelict in the depot for a few years until finally being scrapped. *(MMT)*

Actually, the first post war bus to go into service after the war was number 102 (EN 8536), a Leyland PD1 with the semi-austerity body that Roe was building at the time which is pictured on the right. Number 102 was also withdrawn in 1958 and also lay derelict for a time before being scrapped. *(MMT)*

Pictured lower right is number 119 (EN 8813), one of 13 more Leyland PD1s and PD1As, this time with Northern Counties bodies which arrived in 1946/7, standing in Knowsley Street after working a morning peak journey. It would last until 1963 before being withdrawn and scrapped. *(MMT)*

Among the 1947 deliveries were four Leyland Tiger PS1 single-deckers with 35-seat rear-entrance bodies by Roe, which initially went to work on the Ramsbottom and Rawtenstall routes. Later they were rebuilt with front entrances for one-person-operation of the Heywood local services. Number 133 (EN 8827) is pictured (upper) in its original condition standing on Rochdale Road opposite the depot. The building behind is part of the former Bury Corporation electricity works which supplied the tramways and is still largely unchanged. *(DBC)*

The remainder of the 1947 deliveries were 15 Leyland PD1As with Weymann bodies. One of these, 136 (EN 9036), is shown in the lower picture in Moss Street working a peak hour short journey to Heap Bridge on the Rochdale service. *(SGC)*

Co-ordination and nationalisation

With the end of the war the subject of co-ordination once again reared its head and on 20th June 1945 the Municipal Passenger Transport Association convened a conference in Manchester, attended by representatives of all the municipal transport operators in the area, to consider the best way to secure this in the planning of post-war passenger transport, in regard to future satellite towns, new housing estates and new industries. A Joint Transport Advisory Committee was set up comprising representatives of Ashton-under-Lyne, Bolton, Bury, Manchester, Oldham, Rochdale and Stockport Corporations and the SHMD Transport Board.

Bury, while agreeing to the principal of co-operation, feared domination by Manchester. Alderman Lord, the Chairman of the Finance Committee, contended that it was a plot by Manchester to swallow up the surrounding undertakings and, despite reassurances that there was no intention to do this, commented that he was reminded of the smile on the face of the tiger.

However, it all came to nothing as, at the General Election on 5th July 1945, a Labour Government committed to the nationalisation of all means of production and distribution, was elected by a large majority. The municipal undertakings did not foresee a problem, assuming that nationalisation would only apply to private companies such as Ribble. However, as details of the draft Transport Bill came out it became apparent that its scope would be far wider than anyone had ever thought. The Bill proposed a British Transport Commission to oversee all means of transport, all passenger transport undertakings being transferred to a number of Area Transport Boards. Bury Corporation, like the other municipalities in the area, was happy to consider voluntary co-ordination of certain conditions, but there was no way it would willingly give up control of its local transport.

Mr T Smalley, the General Manager of Barrow-in-Furness Corporation Transport Department, spoke on the matter in a speech about Bury's part in the growth of Lancashire as an industrial county at a luncheon meeting in the Derby Hall. "Nobody knows what will happen to the Bury Transport system," he said. "I should feel sorry if Bury lost its identity in any way as the government of Bury has been such that it commends itself to others." He considered that if local transport undertakings were to be governed by Whitehall there could be a bigger fiasco than that seen in the coal industry during the recent months.

The Government was not swayed by any arguments and the Bill subsequently became the Road Traffic Act 1947, becoming law on 1st January 1948. Although nationalisation of the private bus companies happened fairly quickly, the draft proposals for a Northern Area Transport Board were not published for nearly two years. Shortly afterwards, on 23rd February 1950, another General Election resulted in the Government being returned with an unworkably small majority.

In September 1951 Mr H Jenkinson, the Political Secretary of the Manchester and Salford Co-operative Party, alleged that there was enormous waste in running buses in the Manchester area and urged that a co-ordinated regional transport system should be considered covering Manchester and the neighbouring towns and Urban Districts.

"This," he said, "would enable a reduction in the number of highly paid chief officials and economies could be effected in office work, printing, advertising and administrative buildings"Joining the fight against increased fares the Party alleged a waste of seating capacity, manpower, and petrol, to say nothing of wear and tear and proposed a substantial reduction in the mileage run by empty buses with very few passengers.

Faced with mounting unpopularity in a population that had endured a period of austerity and rationing as long as the war itself, the Government again went to the country and on 25th October 1951 was swept from power. While nationalisation remained, the scheme for area boards was quietly dropped and despite rumblings from time to time was not to be resurrected until the plans for Conurbation Transport Executives some 15 years later.

Heywood local services

In February 1946 Heywood Council discussed the matter of bus services in areas of the town that were currently unserved and resolved that 'This Council is of the opinion it is incumbent upon the Transport Committee to provide travelling facilities to the citizens who reside in the out districts of the Borough. In consequence of their inability to do this, due to high costs, it is imperative that alternative measures be adopted to overcome this difficulty in order that people in the districts affected may enjoy the amenities they are entitled to expect. Therefore we instruct the Committee to enter into immediate negotiations with the Corporation whose bus services operate within the Borough with a view to taking over our service in its entirety, an annual sum to be paid to Heywood Corporation for the privilege of running into the Borough'.

Supporting the motion, Councillor Barrett said that everyone agreed that such districts should be served by public transport. However, Heywood could not run the service as their transport was in the hands of other Corporations. That Heywood would be surrendering its birthright was a stupid argument and he wanted to know if the Transport Committee would be prepared to provide these services if this motion was defeated. It was then agreed that Bury should be asked to run a service, the routes, times, fares and stops to be stipulated by the Heywood Transport Committee on the understanding that any profit or loss would accrue to Heywood, that the service would be operated for a trial period of three months and that application should be made to the Traffic Commissioners without delay.

In March 1946 Bury ran a bus over the proposed routes with officials of both authorities as passengers, following which an application was made to the Traffic Commissioners for two of the three services and possibly the third at some date in the future. The three proposals were:

A circular route from Heywood Town Centre (Bamford Road) to Broadfield Station via Pilsworth Road, returning via Egerton Street and Hind Hill Street.

From the Town Centre to Peel Estate via Bamford Road, Claybank Street and Furness Avenue.

From the Town Centre to Heap Bridge via Bury Old Road and Heap Brow.

While the first two routes were agreed to be suitable, the Heap Bridge route posed problems due the road being too narrow in parts for a bus to pass other traffic, nor was it possible to provide a suitable turning point anywhere along the route. Further, the low railway bridge over Heap Brow would restrict the route to single-deck operation, so in April 1946 it was agreed to defer its introduction. Bury was also short of suitable vehicles to operate the new routes in Heywood and a proposal was made that a single-deck bus should be hired. However, on 5th August 1946 double-deck buses took over the Whitefield-Unsworth-Blackford Bridge route, freeing single-deckers to work in Heywood, service 47 running across the town between Peel Estate and Pilsworth Road from that date.

In October 1946 a petition was received by Heywood Council from the residents of Bury Old Road and Top o' th' Heap for a bus service. This time the Chairman of the Traffic Commissioners visited the district and toured the route, after which he stated that he did not consider Bury Old Road suitable for Public Service Vehicles, but that the Commissioners might be prepared to consider an application if the road was improved. After the intervention of Mr Tony Greenwood, Heywood's Member of Parliament, the necessary improvements were agreed and Councillor Wardle, the Chairman of the Passenger Transport Committee, told Heywood Council in February 1948 that it was proposed to spend £1,400 on alterations to part of the roadway.

After two years of continuous negotiations and the road having been improved, the service commenced on 11th October 1948. It was operated as part of the Heywood Circular route and ran hourly. In 1954 the four Leyland PS1 single-deckers delivered in 1947 were converted for one-person-operation by Northern Counties by moving the entrance to the front immediately behind the driver and were used on the service until their withdrawal in 1962 when they were replaced by AEC Reliances dating from 1957. The service, numbered 48, was eventually extended through to Bury Town Centre.

The end of the trams

The last remaining tram services to Tottington and Walmersley would have been replaced by buses during 1939 if the war had not intervened. However, they had had to continue running with minimal maintenance for another decade. Much discussion ensued in Council on the merits and demerits of trolleybuses but in the end it was decided to convert the services to diesel buses as the cost of replacing the worn-out overhead, much of which had been in continual use since 1904, was prohibitive.

So just after 11 o'clock on the night of Sunday 15th February 1948, after nearly 44 years of faithful and regular service, the last tram from Tottington made its way back to depot. This reversed the events of 15th September 1904 when the then Chairman of the District Council, Councillor Wood, drove the first car from Tottington boundary to the terminus. On this occasion Councillor C Mills, the current Chairman, rode on the platform to the boundary alongside driver Sidney Dorset, waving to the cheering residents. Some leaned out of their windows along the route while others stood on the pavement waving and singing "Auld Lang Syne". Conductor John Hopkins was on duty collecting the last few pennies that the Tottington trams would earn for the Corporation and Inspector Ernest Howard was on the tram checking the tickets issued.

The tram was number 13, one of Bury's first bogie cars dating back to 1903 and by then 45 years old. When it arrived at the Market Place it just went silently to depot with no ceremony. In a tribute to the Tottington trams Councillor Mills said, "All those who used the trams will view their departure with mixed feelings, some with a sense of loss. Though a single track with loops had not helped the efficiency of the service and there had been many aggravating delays, the tramway had played its part in the social life of Tottington and Bury in long memorable years of peace and during the war" Councillor Mills continued, "One of the things which Tottington people will remember with affection is the time during the Second World War when, after a disturbing night in which the war came to Tottington, the old Tottington tramcar, with its unfailing regularity, trundled up to the village in the early morning hours. It was a reassuring sight and sound. I am happy to place on record thanks on behalf of the Urban District Council and residents to all who have, through the tramways, contributed to the service of the community."

At first the replacement buses turned at Tottington by reversing into Kirklees Street, but later a turning circle was built on the corner of Kirklees Street and Market Street.

One of the trams made redundant by the conversion of the Tottington route was the 1903 open-top car which had been rebuilt in 1926 with a fully enclosed body and a new EMB truck and General Electric motors to work on the Heywood to Manchester service, then taking the number 30. In December 1948 it was sold to Sunderland Corporation to work on its extended Durham Road route. Painted green with the mandatory 'Shop at Binns' adverts at either end and fitted with a pantograph instead of a trolley boom it became Sunderland number 85, lasting in service there until 1953.

Now only the Walmersley tram route was left and despite the decision of the Town Council that there was to be no celebration to mark the end of Bury's 46-year-old electric tram service and the end of 66 years of rail transport throughout the town's streets, more than 1,500 residents along the route turned out on the night of Sunday 13th February 1949 to say goodbye. Representatives of the Council stayed away, only two Councillors riding on the tram and only one senior official of the Corporation; Mr LeFevre, the Transport Manager.

At 10.50pm there was the usual quiet atmosphere of a Sunday night at Walmersley terminus, but a few minutes later trams were arriving fully loaded, passengers were alighting from private cars, householders were gathering along the pavement and children were peeping through the bedroom window curtains. Several hundred people had to be prevented by the police from blocking the road when the last tram was seen breasting Pigs Lee Brow at 11 o'clock. Again, it was number 13 which trundled to a standstill. The waiting crowd cheered and sang while passengers scrambled to get on board. The tram was not decorated for the occasion but the words 'BURY'S LAST TRAM 13th FEBRUARY 1949' had been painted on the lower deck windows. It was rumoured that Mr leFevre himself had supplied the white paint. Crowded to capacity, the tram left many intending passengers behind, amongst them Councillor G Schofield who at the previous Council meeting had argued unsuccessfully that a celebration should be held. Driver Gilbert Douglas had a crowded platform for that last journey. There was Christopher Farrar, a veteran driver of 85 who had retired from the Department at the age of 72, Mr LeFevre, Albert Heyes, one of the first half dozen men to be employed by the Tramways Department in 1903,

When the war ended Bury was still running a regular tram service between Tottington and Walmersley through the town centre. In addition, there were still some peak hour journeys along Knowsley Street and Manchester Road along tracks which had been retained mainly for football traffic. The two 4-wheel cars, numbers 30 and 38, which generally worked this service were soon withdrawn leaving just 17 trams remaining, numbers 1-14, rebuilt from the original cars dating back to 1903 and 57/9 and 60, the latest cars new in 1925.

Trams last ran between Bury and Tottington on the evening of Saturday 15th February 1948, buses replacing them the following day. In the picture above, taken in May 1947, passengers board tram number 57 at the Market Place to travel home to Tottington. The building on the left is the former Transport Department Offices. *(ADPC)*

Although the tram pictured at the bottom of the opposite page standing at Walmersley terminus in 1946 is showing Jericho on the front, it is actually about to leave for Tottington, the blind having obviously been set for the benefit of the photographer. Car number 11 was one of the 1903 trams, originally open-top but heavily re-built over the years. *(DBC)*

Above, similar cars 8 and 10 stand together in the Market Place with The Rock behind and the Parish Church out of the picture to the left. Number 8 is on its way along Bolton Street to Tottington while number 10 will go along The Rock to Walmersley Road. *(DBC)*

Tramway operation came to an end on Saturday 13th February 1949 when car number 13, which had run the last journey to Tottington twelve months previously, also worked the last journey on the Walmersley route. Number 13 is pictured right at Walmersley. *(SGC)*

Harry Ashton, Chief Assistant and on the staff for forty-two years, George Edwards, the Traffic Superintendent with forty years service with the Department and GW Mitchell, the Assistant Engineer.

Throughout the journey people darted in front of the tram and put coins on the rails to be flattened for souvenirs. Passengers were in high spirits during the slow journey of 35 minutes to the Town Centre and sang almost all the way. High spirits took a more material form with some of the passengers. Transport Department staff had carefully guarded the vehicle at Walmersley to make sure no practical joker could derail the trolley or do further damage to the already battered coachwork but in the crowded car two conductors were unable to stop souvenir hunters from cutting off the leather strap hanger loops to take home as mementos of the occasion.

As the tram passed Seedfield, bedroom windows were lit up and pyjama-clad householders watched crowds assembled at the stopping point. At Chesham Road another crowd of people was waiting to applaud the procession and more sightseers crowded the upper windows of the Cobden Club. Along The Rock the passengers struck up 'Auld Lang Syne' and managed to make the last line coincide with the tram stopping outside the Derby Hotel, the spot from which the first steam tram had set out 66 years earlier.

Number 13 arrived outside the Derby Hotel just after 11.35pm but was unable to move off again for nearly 20 minutes. Then about 50 people decided they would see the tram home and as midnight sounded by the Parish Church clock, the last Bury tram rumbled off along Princess Street towards the depot. It was reported that nearly 500 passengers were carried on the round trip to Walmersley and back, but attempts to get the last ticket did not end when the trams emptied in the Town Centre. The last passenger to get on board was a man waiting at the corner of Rochdale Road and Princess Street who rode only a hundred yards for his penny fare. But even he did not get the last ticket as that was purchased by the Transport Manager Mr LeFevre, as the tram approached the depot doors. Bury's tramways were no more.

The following morning at 5.10am the first bus on the Walmersley route left Bury displaying the route number 30. After the last tram had run a local poet put his thoughts into verse and composed these lines.

'Farewell good pal, it's cheerio at last,
A friend to me you have been in the past.
In good weather and bad you have brought me home.
I'll never forget your red white and chrome.
Via Moorgate, Chesham, Limefield and Walmersley,
We have travelled the King's Highway.
So for Auld Lang Syne I bid thee farewell,
And drink your good health to-day.
Farewell!'

Number 154 (EN 9554) was one of five Weymann-bodied Leyland PD2/4s which were purchased to replace the Walmersley trams. They were also Bury's first buses built to the new maximum width of 8ft. Number 154 is pictured leaving Moss Street for Rochdale on service 21. *(MMT)*

Buses to Nangreaves

As far back as 1936 there had been requests from residents for a service up Walmersley Old Road to the small hamlet of Nangreaves, but they had always been turned down due to the narrowness of the road. After the war further requests were made for a service to Nangreaves and finally Councillors inspected the road and suggested that a bus might run as far as the Masons Arms at Baldingstone, the sharp S-bend just past there making it difficult for a bus to negotiate especially when ice or snow covered the road.

However, the older residents of Nangreaves still thought there was a case for some form of bus service, arguing that because of the long walk up from the Walmersley tram terminus shopping in Bury took all day and a service on Fridays and Saturdays would be sufficient. They were not amused by a remark by Councillor Farrar, the Chairman of the Transport Committee, that people who chose to live in the middle of a field should provide their own transport.

Eventually, the Committee bowed to the pressure and purchased two little petrol-engined Guy Wolfs with 20-seat bodies by Barnards of Norwich, which it is believed were originally ordered by South Shields Corporation and were acquired at a bargain price. These smart little

vehicles, which became known locally as the 'Nanny Fliers' were numbered 149 and 150 and operated the service for six years until road widening allowed full size single-deckers to be used. The service, numbered 49, started on 2nd July 1948 and picked up additional revenue by serving the densely populated area along Hornby Street, to the west of Walmersley Road, which was also too narrow for conventional buses. They were also used on the Calrows route and were withdrawn in December 1954, 149 becoming the Departments maintenance lorry in which role it lasted until 1961.

The next new buses, 25 Leyland PD2/4 Titans with Weymann 56-seat bodies numbered 151-175 arrived between May 1949 and March 1950 and replaced the last trams and left only 12 pre-war buses in the fleet.

Having finally agreed to running to Nangreaves the problem then arose of what buses to use. Two petrol-engine Guy Wolfs with Barnard bodies were purchased, the choice believed to be influenced by their being an order cancelled by South Shields Corporation and as such being readily available at a knock-down price. Number 150 (EN 9181) is seen above in Moss Street. It was withdrawn in 1954 and passed to Bury Corporation Health Department, eventually becoming a mobile shop in Heywood. *(SGC)*

THE FIFTIES

Light at the end of the tunnel

The decade of the fifties began very much as an anticlimax. After five drab years of post war austerity people were looking forward to the second half of the century for a return to better things, but unfortunately for the transport industry in general it signalled the beginning of a long downward spiral of falling patronage and rising costs. It started with most bus operators at a low point with a shortage of buses and a lengthy wait for new orders to be delivered. Bury, having got in early, was better off than most, but there was still rationing and Government control of just about everything needed to rebuild the business. The private car was beginning to make inroads into passenger levels and in a labour-intensive industry such as bus operation costs soared out of all proportion to those in manufacturing.

For a short period the Walshaw service was extended along High Street towards Ainsworth as far as Dow Lane to serve the military personnel housed in the army huts on Lowercroft Road, but due to the difficult reverse it was extended further to turn round in the yard of the Lowercroft Mill. When the facility was closed in April 1956 the service reverted to its original terminus in Walshaw village.

By the end of 1950 the four Burlingham-bodied Leyland Tiger single-deckers dating from 1938 were surplus to requirements, but the Department was unable to find a buyer. So the torque converters were removed and the chassis were converted to TD5s and despatched to Massey Brothers of Wigan from where they emerged in November 1951 with new 56-seat double-deck bodies. In this form they ran in Bury for another seven years before further service elsewhere.

On 3rd December 1952 a short route started along Woodhill Road to Calrows. Numbered 53, it was a single-deck service due to the low bridge under the Holcombe Brook railway line and was one-man operated from the start.

The general gloom was gradually lifting and the Coronation of the young Queen Elizabeth II on 2nd June 1953 heralded a period of optimism; the new Elizabeth age. In the same year the Transport Department celebrated its Golden Jubilee and to honour the occasion a dinner was held in the Derby Hall in Market Street on the evening of Tuesday 30th June. Members of Manchester and Heywood Transport Committees were also invited along with some of the employees and others who had retired after long service with the Department.

The first AECs to join the Bury fleet for nearly twenty years entered service in October 1952. These were two Regent IIIs with Weymann 56-seat rear entrance bodies and were numbered 176 and 177. They were followed by nine identical Weymann bodies mounted on Leyland PD2/3 chassis which were delivered in May and June the following year, their numbers being 178-186.

In March 1956 Mr LeFevre resigned to take up the appointment of General Manager and Engineer of Halifax Passenger Transport Department. His successor at Bury was Mr Frank Thorp. Mr Thorp was 42 years old and Chief Engineer of Nottingham City Transport Department where he had been since 1953. A native of South Manchester, he was educated at Manchester Grammar School, joining Manchester Corporation Transport Department as a clerk in the Chief Engineer's Office and later becoming a draughtsman. In 1940 he enlisted in the Royal Corps of Signals, his military service taking him to North Africa, Italy and Germany, reaching the rank of Major. In April 1946 he returned to Manchester as Chief Draughtsman and was later promoted to Chief Technical Officer. He moved to Salford City Transport as a Technical Engineer in 1948 and on to Nottingham five years later. A married man with two sons, this was Mr Thorp's first managerial post which he took up in June 1956.

Two well-known members of the Department retired in 1956. One was Sam Madden who had worked as a conductor for 37 years after returning from service in the First World War. He began his career as a tram conductor on the Heywood route and later worked for many years on the trams to Walmersley and Tottington. He transferred to the Heywood Circular route in 1946, the day that the service started, and worked on it for ten years. Known as the 'Chirpy Conductor' he was presented with a number of gifts by his fellow employees, passengers on the route and the employees of the Unity Mills at Broadfield.

The other was Arthur Williams, who had been a maintenance mechanic in the Department. In his spare time he was quite an artist and he would

The final 16 buses of the 1949 order arrived in the first three months of 1950. They were numbered 160-75 and were more Weymann-bodied Leyland Titan PD2/4s. Number 172 (EN 9972) is pictured above swinging out of Moss Street into Market Street on its way to Walmersley on service 30 which had replaced the trams the previous year. *(MMT)*

Pictured below is number 74 (EN 7703) which began life in 1938 as number 75, one of four Leyland Tiger TS8cs with Burlingham single-deck bodies. In 1951 they were converted to TD5s, fitted with manual gearboxes and gained new double-deck bodies by Massey Brothers of Wigan. It was withdrawn in 1958 and passed to Paton of Renfrew where it ran for another six years. It is seen in Haymarket Street working on service 1 to Walshaw. *(RM)*

Number 176 (BEN 176), in the upper picture, was one of a pair of AEC Regent III, the chassis of which had been stored at Bury for several years. They finally went into service in 1952 with 56-seat bodies by Weymann. Both buses survived long enough to be taken into the SELNEC fleet in 1969 and took the fleet numbers 6376/7 although neither received the orange livery. *(MMT)*

In 1953 Bury took delivery of nine Leyland Titan PD2/3s with identical bodies to the two Regents. In the lower picture number 180 (BEN 180) stands in Moss Street alongside the Kay Gardens while working on service 9 to Jericho. Number 180 also went to SELNEC and along with number 186 spent its last days at Stalybridge. *(DBC)*

quite often pin up a drawing he had done of a particular event that had happened in the depot. He was a prolific creator of cartoons and children's drawings all his life and his drawings had been reproduced in newspapers, magazines and books all over the country. One of his early commissions was a regular football cartoon in the local paper, the 'Bury Guardian'. As part of his education he had attended Bury Art School and his work as an artist included drawings and captioning the slogans on Bury Road Safety Committee calendars which he did for fourteen years.

Bigger buses

A significant development took place in July 1956 when the Ministry of Transport increased the maximum permitted length of double-deck buses to 30ft. The following month the Transport Committee recommended that a 30ft double-deck bus should be tried out and tested on routes around the town. In October a Leyland Atlantean demonstrator, one of only three prototypes in existence, was borrowed for a week's trial. The new bus was 30ft long, seated 78 passengers, was air-conditioned and had the entrance at the front with the engine at the rear.

After the bus's visit to Bury, Mr Thorp said, "Both the members of the Transport Committee and the Departments employees made some valuable suggestions that will be forwarded to the manufacturers" Mr Thorp continued, "I am very impressed by the new vehicle, which was first introduced to the public at the Commercial Motor Show at Earl's Court. The design is unconventional, but if nobody was prepared to try out unconventional designs there would be no progress. The chief advantage of this new bus is its seating capacity, compared with 56 on the conventional 27ft long double-decker. This makes it possible to carry larger loads at lower costs. The wide single-step entrance and short staircases will speed up loading and unloading, making faster schedules possible. The disadvantage of earlier types of 30ft double-deck buses was that the conductor had so many fares to collect he was unable to supervise the platform properly. In the new model with the entrance at the front, the driver supervises the loading and unloading from the cab and the conductor can concentrate solely on collecting fares. The driver has finger-tip control of the electro-pneumatic gearbox with only two pedals, brake and accelerator. The bus is fitted with power operated doors controlled by the driver, a feature which will reduce accidents by preventing passengers from boarding or alighting while the bus is moving or at traffic lights. I consider there is no vehicle which offers greater prospects of future development. It represents the best effort yet to solve the problem facing every transport undertaking in these days of high overheads; how to secure the maximum economy while maintaining an efficient service to the public."

However, at the time the Atlantean was still a step too far, but in March 1957 the people of Bury had an opportunity to ride in a more conventional 30ft double deck bus. This was the Potteries Motor Traction Company's 700 AEH, a Leyland PD3 Titan with an MCW Orion 74-seat rear-entrance lightweight body which was borrowed and used for a week as a demonstration vehicle on routes to Bolton and Rochdale. These buses generally had a reputation for hard riding when lightly loaded and being short on power when full, but it would appear that Bury was more impressed than some other operators as orders were placed for 25 similar vehicles although with the added refinement of platform doors electrically operated by the driver.

But improvements in design were not confined to double-deckers. On 1st April 1957 six 30ft long under-floor-engined AEC Reliance single-deckers with 43-seat Weymann bodies arrived for one-person services. They were numbered 81-86 and were used to convert services 20 Ainsworth-Radcliffe-Whitefield and 8 Unsworth-Whitefield to one-person-operation, the latter being extended to Bury and renumbered 38 at the same time. Numbers 81 and 82 were fitted with high-speed rear axles for use on private hire work when required.

The first ten 30ft double-deckers arrived in April 1958. Numbered 201-210, they were Leyland PD3/6s with Weymann-badged 73-seat bodies, 32 in the lower saloon and 41 on the upper deck. A revised front indicator layout was fitted, with larger route numbers below a single destination blind and no via blind. There was an emergency door at the rear, on the platform at the bottom of the stairs. The livery was a little different with the front dome painted cream instead of green as before. Ten more were delivered in September 1958 as 211-220 and the final five, 221-225 in March 1959.

The PD3s all came with rear wheel hub covers but after a few weeks were suffering from overheated rear wheels. The discs were modified in several ways to try to get more air to the hub but with no appreciable effect and eventually they were removed and the problem went away.

Technical developments

But there were more pressing matters as, in November 1956, the Egyptian government of President Gamal Abdul Nasser had closed the Suez Canal and precipitated a fuel crisis as tankers from the Gulf now had to travel all the way round the southern tip of Africa to bring oil to Europe. In Britain fuel rationing was once more imposed and most bus operators cut services, mainly in the off peak and at weekends. Bury, however, escaped the worst effects as some months earlier Mr Thorp had been experimenting with coaline, an indigenous fuel which was not rationed and could be mixed with normal diesel oil in order to make financial economies and to provide a safeguard for supplies. His intention was to introduce it gradually but the scheme was hurriedly brought forward. The buses ran on a mixture of 20% coaline and 80% diesel, thereby saving the department up to one fifth of its imported fuel oil. Practically the entire bus fleet was running on this mixture.

Up to 1947 Bell Punch type pre-printed tickets had been used on Bury trams and buses, but in that year TIM machines, which printed directly on to plain paper rolls, were introduced bringing with them major savings in ticket costs and office staff.

When the Reliances arrived for one-person-operation in April 1957, they were equipped with 'Ultimate' ticket machines, each containing six rolls of small pre-printed tickets of different values. The machines were slotted into a cradle on the cab door of the Reliances or on a shelf to the left of the driver on PS1s 130-133. Change-giving machines were also mounted in the cabs to the left of the driver.

In the early 1960s Mr Thorp designed an innovative ticket issuing machine containing a roll of some 1,500 pre-printed tickets interwound with an audit roll, the machine punching out the values and fare stages not required. The audit ribbon was retained in the ticket machine and then passed through an accounting machine which used compressed air to trigger off counters as the ribbon was passed through. Three machines and one counter were produced by the firm of Creed and Company Ltd and were tried out by various operators, but the ticket roll and audit ribbon were thin and the punch needles were delicate and the machine never reached the production stage.

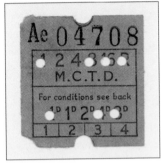

Very few examples of a Creed ticket are known to have survived. This one was issued by Manchester Corporation for a 3d fare from stage 6. The ticket was pink. *(CR)*

Recasting the network

During 1957 Mr Thorp put forward a scheme for linking a number of Bury's busiest and most frequent bus routes to create cross town services, the aim being to cut down on dead mileage and help alleviate congestion in the area around Kay Gardens. The first pair of services selected was 7 to Whitefield and 30 to Walmersley which were linked as 37 Whitefield to Walmersley running along the busy north to south A56 road through the town. Simply by cutting out the number of circuits of the Kay Gardens triangle alone, a saving of 187 miles a week was anticipated, equivalent to 9,700 miles a year. The new service commenced on 13th January 1958.

A month later Mr Thorp put forward detailed proposals for linking another eight services to form a full cross-town network. These comprised the routes to Ainsworth, Alfred Street, Bolton, Jericho, Radcliffe, Rochdale, Tottington and Walshaw. It was estimated that the full scheme would save 35,500 miles a year. Figures produced at that time showed that in one hour in the peak period 126 buses used Haymarket Street, 93 used Moss Street and 88 used Market Street. By linking routes and re-routing the new services the traffic density could be cut to 57 using Haymarket Street, 23 using Moss Street and 39 using Market street. The proposals involved quite a few alterations to bus stops around Kay Gardens and the side streets in the town centre.

With the move to one-person-operation Bury purchased six single-deckers in 1957. These were AEC Reliances with 43-seat front-entrance bodies by Weymann and were the first underfloor-engined buses in the fleet. In the upper picture number 83 (FEN 83) travels out of Bury along Haymarket Street on the way to Whitefield on the newly converted service 38.

The 25 Leyland Titan PD3/6s, delivered in 1958/9, were arguably the best known of Bury's buses. Number 209 (GEN 209) is seen in the lower picture standing outside the Town Hall on Knowsley Street as it arrived in Bury from Stopes on service 16. It became SELNEC 6359 and was withdrawn in 1974 passing to a Scottish bingo club. *(Both SGC)*

However, the Committee wanted time to assess the operation of the Whitefield to Walmersley route. This was deemed successful as the following year a further three new cross-town services were created. Bury's first bus route, 1 to Walshaw, was linked to 25 to Radcliffe as 1, 2 to Ainsworth was extended to Alfred Street incorporating 28 and 9 to Jericho ran through to and from Tottington over the 33 route. In most cases short workings on either side continued to use the old number. All three started on 16th March 1959. The proposal to join Bolton (23T) with Rochdale (21T) was abandoned as neither Bolton nor Rochdale Corporations were in favour.

For some years requests had been received for service 52, which still followed the original tram route through Radcliffe along Spring Lane and Water Street, to go into the Bus Station which was nearer the shops and the Market Hall. Both Radcliffe Council and the local Chamber of Trade supported the requests on the grounds that it would bring people into the town centre to shop rather than going to Bolton or Bury. However, Mr Thorp stated that the re-routing would cost an extra bus and as the service was already operating at a loss he could not agree to the suggestion.

At the end of the decade the large new Bolton Road housing estate was built west of Radcliffe to the north of the road to Stopes and Little Lever. The residents there also had designs on service 52 and petitioned Radcliffe Council for it to be diverted through the estate. but Bury rejected this for the same reason that it had turned down the previous request. However, after more pressure, Bury eventually agreed to run a service round the estate. A new service 65 commenced in August 1960 and was co-ordinated with service 5 (Whitefield to Ainsworth via Goats Gate), but was later routed along Stand Lane to terminate at Hollinhurst Road. On 18th June 1962 it was extended to Whitefield Bus Station via Ringley Road and Church Lane. Over the years various alterations were made also involving services 5, 15 and 20.

During 1959 Leyland Atlantean demonstrator 398 JTB was borrowed and early the following year Daimler's Fleetline demonstrator 7000 HP, painted in Birmingham deep blue and cream, came to Bury for a few days.

The Daimler Fleetline demonstrator 7000 HP, which was on trial in Bury early in 1960, is pictured while working on Manchester Corporation's service 40 during the same period. *(CR)*

THE LAST TEN YEARS

Lenny

Most people think of the 1960s as the swinging sixties; a time when Britain finally broke away from the shackles of rationing and controls. It was an exciting time with new fashions, new designs and new freedoms, but it was also a period when wage inflation started to soar and the viability of the bus industry began to deteriorate. The vicious downward spiral of rising costs, fare increases and loss of passengers, followed by further fare increases, gathered momentum. Services were pruned back but fixed costs remained substantially the same and more income had to be raised from fewer and fewer passengers. Staff shortages were also starting to cause problems as a job on the buses with its relatively low wages and unsociable hours became less and less attractive compared to new jobs in developing industries. Against this background momentous changes would occur which would bring about the end of Bury Transport Department's independent existence.

In December 1960 Bury Corporation made a little bit of history when it received the first Guy Wulfrunian to go into service with a British municipal transport undertaking after it had been exhibited on the Guy stand at the Commercial Motor Show two months earlier. The Wulfrunian, the local name for a resident of Wolverhampton where it was built, was quoted as being the most advanced design of double deck bus on the British market, costing in the region of £7,000. It was 30ft long with 73 seats and although only 13ft 4in high had the normal upper deck seating layout with central gangway. The entrance was at the front with the stairs going upwards to the rear over the front near-side wheel. The engine was the then new 135hp Gardner 6LX which was also placed at the front between the platform and the driving position but off-set towards the offside of the chassis to create a larger platform area. The transmission was of the pneumocyclic semi-automatic type, fairly new for buses at that time, with the gear selector switch on an arm on the left of the steering column. It was also unusual in having air suspension (by Firestone) and disc brakes (by Girling) on all four wheels. The body was badged as Park Royal, but was erected by Charles Roe at Leeds.

The bus was formally handed over to Councillor W Alker, the Chairman of the Transport Committee, on Tuesday 6th December, 1960 at a ceremony on the forecourt of the Town Hall with chassis, engine and bodymakers' representatives in attendance. After the ceremony the Mayor, Councillor JC Kenyon, members of the Transport Committee, Corporation Officials and representatives of the manufacturers and trade unions attended a luncheon at the Normandie Hotel at Birtle, the journey to Birtle being made in the new bus. The Mayor stated that he was very impressed with the vehicle's riding qualities as they came up the rather difficult road. "I think it rode excellently up here and I hope it is going to be a great success in our fleet." he declared. Councillor Alker commented that by putting this new bus into service it would increase the safety of the passengers. By having a front entrance, the driver would be able to watch everybody safely on and off the platform and no matter what state the town's roads might be in the bus would float along. The undertaking was facing intense competition from many other forms of transport and the Department would have to go out and meet that competition. Some way, traffic had to be attracted back to the buses and one way was to be bold in experimenting.

The new bus was given the fleet number 101 and registered LEN 101, so it was hardly surprising that it was quickly christened 'Lenny' by the workforce. However, it was not a popular vehicle with either crews or passengers and underwent many modifications by the manufacturers both in their own workshops and at Bury depot.

Lenny stayed at Bury for less than three years and in October 1963 it was sold to Howells and Withers, of Pontllanfraith, Monmouthshire, later passing to Wright of Wrexham and then to Berresfords of Cheddleton, Staffordshire. By mid 1971 it was out of service at the back of Berresford's yard, remaining there in an ever-deteriorating condition until 1982 when it joined the buses in the Greater Manchester Museum of Transport at Boyle Street, Cheetham Hill.

The Wulfrunian was ahead of its time and only 137 were ever built, the combination of high development costs and low sales contributing to the demise of Guy as a bus manufacturer.

Number 101 (LEN 101) was the first Wulfrunian to go into service with a municipal operator when it arrived at Bury in December 1960. The body was built by Charles H Roe at Leeds on a Park Royal frame and the bus is pictured outside the Roe factory before delivery. The design was ahead of its time and number 101 only ran for three years, mostly out of service, before doing the rounds of several small operators until it eventually came into the possession of the Greater Manchester Museum of Transport. *(MMT)*

The next purchases were far more satisfactory; fifteen standard Leyland Atlanteans with robust Metro-Cammell bodies which passed to the SELNEC PTE and lasted up to 20 years. Number 115 (REN 115) pauses in Moss Street on its way from Whitefield to Walmersley on service 37. *(SGC)*

More trouble in Heywood

After the war Manchester City Council embarked on a programme of building huge overspill housing estates on the outer edges of the conurbation to re-house people from the crowded inner city areas. In the early 1960s it bought a large area of land to the west of Heywood town centre and to the south of Bury Old Road, and when it started to build what was to become Darn Hill the can of worms was well and truly opened. Manchester had run its buses into Heywood from the Middleton direction since taking over the Middleton Electric Traction Company's route in 1925, and three years later had run its Norden to Gatley express service across the town centre and along Bamford Road, but Bury had always considered the west side of Heywood to be its territory. In 1946 it had started its Heywood local service along Pilsworth Road and by 1948 it was running its service 48 along Bury Old Road, which was the northern boundary of the development.

The residents of the new estate had their roots in Manchester and not unreasonably wanted to travel there for work and leisure and not to Bury so Manchester applied to serve Darn Hill by extending its 63 service along Bury Street and Bury Old Road, entering the estate from that direction. Bury's reaction was predictable, demanding a share in the operation as the price of its agreement.

Manchester, however, would not agree to Bury buses working into Manchester through Middleton and down Rochdale Road, and instead applied for a route along Hind Hill Street and Egerton Street which allowed it to enter the estate by Argyle Street. However, these streets were already being used by Bury's Heywood circular service but, after a bitter battle through the Traffic Court, Manchester eventually gained its licence. When it started running an all-day service on the route Bury bowed to the inevitable and on 31st March 1964 reorganised its own services to avoid the area, the best it could achieve being to run the revised 48 service a couple of hundred yards into the estate to a turning circle at the junction of Argyle Street and Sutherland Road. First Manchester later extended the 63 (by then 163) service through to Bury, something which even the PTE had never done.

More big buses

Despite his experience with the Wulfrunian, Mr Thorp remained an advocate of high capacity double-deckers and placed orders for both Leyland and Daimler versions. However, in January 1963, before the first examples arrived in Bury, he resigned to take up the position of General Manager at Newport, which at that time had a fleet of 117 buses compared to Bury's 99. His successor was Mr Norman Kay, the Deputy General Manager at West Bromwich. Born in Ramsbottom, Mr Kay had attended Bury Technical School before starting his career as a junior clerk with Ramsbottom Corporation. Mr Kay took up the post on 1st May 1963 and was to be Bury Corporation Transport Departments last General Manager.

Bury's first Leyland Atlanteans had arrived the month before. Numbered 102-116, they were 15 PDR1/1 models with 74-seat bodies by MCW to a design currently being supplied to Liverpool. They were unusual in having an opening vent in the front nearside windscreen, but a short time after their arrival a flat screen was fitted as the vent obscured the driver's view of the nearside mirror. They were the first Bury buses to be fitted with fluorescent internal lighting. Mounted in the angle between the ceiling and the side, the tubes were covered by a curved panel of opaque plastic so that transparent advertisements could be stuck on and illuminated from behind.

The following year 15 Daimler Fleetlines came into the fleet. Numbered 117-131 they introduced yet another new bodybuilder in Walter Alexander Limited of Falkirk. Bury's bodies had two-piece flat windscreens as opposed to the normal wrap-round, curved screens of that bodybuilder. Two more AEC Reliances, numbers 87 and 88, arrived at the same time. They also had Alexander bodies, this time with the standard curved windscreen, and outwardly were identical but differed in their braking systems, 87 being vacuum operated and 88 using compressed air. Early in 1965 Manchester Corporation Leyland Panther number 76 with a Park Royal 43-seat dual-door body was borrowed and ran mainly on the single-deck routes although it also worked on the Bullfinch Drive route.

A further six Fleetlines were delivered in the spring of 1965, this time with bodies by East Lancashire Coachbuilders. Numbers 132-137

Seventeen buses arrived in 1964 comprising 15 double-deckers and two single-deckers. The former were Daimler Fleetlines with 74-seat bodies from Alexander, a builder new to Bury. The first of these, number 117 (TEN 117) is pictured above in Moss Street while working on service 37 to Walmersley. *(MMT)*

The two single-deckers were AEC Reliances and also carried Alexander bodies, the bus in the picture below, also in Moss Street while working the short one-person route 53 to Calrows, is number 87 (TEN 887). *(DBC)*

For its next orders Bury chose East Lancashire Coachbuilders of Blackburn. In 1965 six Daimler Fleetlines arrived including number 136 (AEN 836C) pictured above outside the art gallery in Moss Street en route for Tottington on service 9. *(SGC)*

Two years later seven buses were delivered. The first three were Daimler Fleetline single-deckers with two door bodies. Number 89 (FEN 89E) stands on The Mosses bus park having previously worked in from Whitefield on service 38. *(SGC)*

The other four buses were Leyland Titan PD2/37s for service 23 where a weight restriction on Trinity Street railway bridge in Bolton precluded the use of larger buses. Number 189 (FEN 589E) is pictured leaving Bury for Bolton. *(MMT)*

had a new design of front destination display consisting of a single aperture containing service number and destination side by side, which could be changed by the driver without leaving his cab.

The introduction of front-entrance buses to the fleet caused the re-siting of some bus stops in and around the town. Stops at street corners that were quite suitable for rear entrance buses caused problems with the newer vehicles blocking the entry into the side streets, especially with one-person-operation increasing the standing time while fares were collected.

In 1965, after a year as vice-President, Alderman William Alker, the Chairman of the Transport Committee, became President of the Municipal Passenger Transport Association, one of the top posts in the public transport world. He was the first Bury man to be elected to the job in the 65 years of the Association's history when, on Thursday 23rd September 1965, he was installed in his office during the annual meeting of the Association at Torquay. The ceremony was watched by Bury's Mayor, Councillor CE Jackson and the Mayoress Mrs M Ashton who, by coincidence, were in Torquay for another conference.

For many years Alderman Alker had been a leading figure in the municipal transport world. He had been an Executive Committee member of the Association for nine years and in 1955/6 he was Chairman of the Association's Area 'C', which comprised 33 transport undertakings in Lancashire and Cheshire.

In his installation speech, Alderman Alker forecast a 'tough time' for municipal transport undertakings but expressed his assurance that the Association and its affiliated organisations would work together towards a solution to prevent any problems. His year involved eight area conferences in different parts of the country and representing the Association at other meetings of public transport undertakings and technical committees. The Transport Committee placed on record its congratulations on Alderman Alker's election as President.

By now service development was restricted to minor infilling and on 15th October 1965 a new shopping service 18 started running to Topping Fold, a small council estate squeezed in between an industrial area, the River Roch and the M66 motorway to the south of Rochdale Old Road.

One-person-operation

Arguably the greatest potential for economy was one-person-operation. Back in 1925 Bury's first services to Ainsworth, Walshaw and Brandlesholme had been operated by the driver only, but as buses and traffic grew conductors were used. In 1954 the four Leyland Tigers, 130-133, were rebuilt with a front entrance for one-person-operation of the Nangreaves and Heywood local services. Three years later the six AEC Reliances were used to convert the Whitefield-Radcliffe-Ainsworth and Bury-Unsworth-Whitefield routes. Then, on 1st July 1966, after a great deal of pressure from the bus operators, the Government finally authorised one-person-operation of double-deckers, although Bury were not to implement this for another three years.

In October 1966, two of Bury's Leyland PD2s were loaned to Oldham Corporation which at that time had a major engineering problem resulting in a shortage of buses. 158 and 159 joined other buses from Bolton, Bradford, Manchester, Rochdale, Salford and Sheffield, Oldham borrowing forty-five buses in all.

The 1967 deliveries comprised three single-deckers and four double-deckers, all bodied by East Lancs. The single-deckers were 33ft long Daimler Fleetlines with 41-seat two-door bodies and room for 19 standees numbered 89-91, but the big surprise was the four double-deckers which were the traditional Leyland Titan PD2/37 model with a forward-entrance 65-seat body. At this time the bridge over the railway at Trinity Street station in Bolton had a weight restriction which prevented large buses using it while fully loaded, so to operate service 23T Bury needed smaller buses and those being used were by now 14 years old. The newcomers took fleet numbers 187-190 carrying on from the older PD2/3s.

As part of the drive to find a suitable vehicle for future one-person-operation two buses were borrowed for evaluation during the year. Both were single-deckers, the first being LYY 827D, a turquoise AEC Swift with Marshall 48-seat two-door body which ran in the town for a few days at the beginning of January. Then in May a blue and white Leyland Panther Cub demonstrator with a 43-seat two-door body by Strachans was tried out.

For a long time there had been requests for some form of service along Chesham Road and it was finally agreed to provide a limited service for the area at shopping times. The new service 32 started running as far as Chester Street on 24th September 1968. Bury Corporation's network was now complete.

The 1968 Transport Act

There had already been three previous attempts to introduce differing degrees of co-ordination and integration of bus services in the Manchester conurbation; the Joint Committee of the twenties, the SELEC scheme of the thirties and the Area Transport Boards in the forties, but none of these had come to fruition. However, with declining traffic and with costs and fares soaring something had to be done before public transport in Britain followed that of America into near oblivion.

During 1962 the Transport Users Consultative Committee was becoming concerned about the position and suggested to operators in the area that 'a full enquiry into the needs of the passenger suburban road and rail services of the Manchester conurbation and South East Lancashire and North East Cheshire generally should be made as a matter of urgency, and that the local authorities and independent bus undertakings in the area should take the initiative and jointly organize a comprehensive survey of all their traffic problems.' Subsequently, in June 1963 a meeting of the interested parties was held in Manchester, but nothing came of it and the following year a left wing Labour Government came to power, with a manifesto committing it to the co-ordination of public transport.

Total nationalisation was no longer a serious political option, so attention was focused on the major conurbations and in 1965 Mrs Barbara Castle, the Minister of Transport, produced a White Paper called 'Transport Policy' which proposed the creation of a number of Conurbation Transport Authorities to plan, manage and finance the operation of local transport within their areas. She saw them also being responsible for land use and highway planning and even car parking policy but this was a step too far and the proposals were watered down.

Now named Passenger Transport Authorities, four were created initially centred on Manchester, Liverpool, Birmingham and Newcastle. Bury

On a wet April day in 1968, a muddy number 142 (HEN 542F) would be only a few days old when it was photographed in Haymarket Street while working on service 21. *(SGC)*

The last buses for Bury Corporation were delivered in 1968.

Three Leyland Atlanteans with East Lancs bodies designed for one-person-operation and painted in the new livery with more cream arrived in the February and went to work on service 29 to Bullfinch Drive on which number 1 (KEN 231G) is seen loading in Moss Street. Number 1 became SELNEC 6391 and was withdrawn in 1982. *(SGC)*

Next, in March and April came six more single-deck Fleetlines, again with East Lancs bodies. Number 92 (KEN 292G) is working the Heywood service soon after delivery. They became SELNEC 6092-7 and later went to Salford where they were allocated to Weaste depot. *(MMT)*

Bury's final bus was number 81 (KEN 381G), a Bedford J2 with body by Willowbrook. Intended for the Chesham route it eventually gravitated to Ramsbottom where it worked a local route until withdrawn in 1976. *(MMT)*

was included in the Manchester authority known by the ponderous title of 'South East Lancashire and North East Cheshire', which was abbreviated to SELNEC. Initially, a small group was set up to look at transport problems in the area and to identify possible solutions. Known as the SELNEC Area Land Use and Transportation Study or SALTS for short, it was largely funded by the Government with contributions from the constituent local authorities.

While Bury, like most other authorities, accepted the need for some form of integration, and indeed amalgamation, they were unhappy that an outside body would be able to set service levels and fares without local consultation, which was exactly the same reason that the SELEC scheme had foundered some thirty years earlier.

After lengthy consultation a further White Paper, 'Public Transport and Planning', was produced in 1967. This proposed a two-tier organisation with a Passenger Transport Authority, consisting of elected members of the constituent authorities, to set policy and a professional Passenger Transport Executive to carry it out. The Executive would acquire the assets of the local authorities and would operate the services. The White Paper became the 1968 Transport Act, which came into force on 1st April 1969, a date that its critics deemed appropriate.

The last months

Although one-person-operation (OPO) of double-deckers had been authorised for almost three years, Bury's first such service did not start until 2nd June 1969 when the Bullfinch Drive route was converted using the newest Fleetlines, 132-137, designed with OPO in mind. To speed fare collection a small number of 'SABLOC' ticket issuing machines was borrowed from Manchester City Transport. Designed by Ken Holt, then Manchester's Chief Accountant, the machine was used exclusively on its OPO services which at the time had a simplified fare structure and a no change policy. Passengers were expected to have the correct fare in either 3d or 6d coins ready when boarding and would put the coins in a slot at the top of the machine and then press a button on the front to issue a ticket of 3d, 6d or 9d. There were problems however; a special non-standard fare table limited to the three fares

was necessary, the internal mechanism was very delicate and suffered many breakdowns; damaged or illegal coins quickly jammed the machine and the cash vault was not big enough. The driver was soon issued with an Ultimate machine to cover all eventualities. The SABLOCs lasted a few months and then were sent back to Manchester and replaced by the much simpler and more reliable 'Johnson' fare box without tickets. However, this system was prone to fraud and loss of revenue and in October 1972 fareboxes were replaced by Bell Punch Solomatic machines.

A small order for six more Daimler Fleetlines arrived in the spring of 1968. These had East Lancs double-deck bodies which were basically the same as the previous batch but with a peaked front dome and a one-piece curved windscreen. They were numbered 138-143.

Bury's last deliveries consisted of ten assorted vehicles which were delivered during 1969. The first three were Leyland Atlanteans with East Lancashire Coachbuilders bodies, specially designed for OPO with two doors and a centre staircase. A periscope was fitted in the cab so that the driver could see the top deck. Painted in a new livery with cream as the dominant colour, they received fleet numbers 1-3.

The two demonstrators had obviously not made a great impression as the next six buses were more 33ft single-deck Fleetlines similar to the three delivered in 1967 and numbered 92-97. They also had a version of the mainly cream livery.

The last bus in the order was the very last one to be delivered to Bury Corporation when it arrived in July 1969. A radical departure, number 81 was a Bedford J2 with Willowbrook/Duple Midland 21-seat body purchased for the Chesham Road route as the heavier buses were considered unsuitable for the roads in the Chesham area. It was the first and only example of both Bedford chassis and this body make in the Bury fleet and was known by the bus crews as 'The Bread Van'.

For a time, while the PTA formulated its strategy, the Council continued to be responsible for day to day operation until the Passenger Transport Executive was formed. Then at midnight on 31st October 1969 Bury Corporation Transport Department ceased to exist. The following morning the undertaking came under the control of the SELNEC PTE, so ending an era of locally governed passenger transport in Bury.

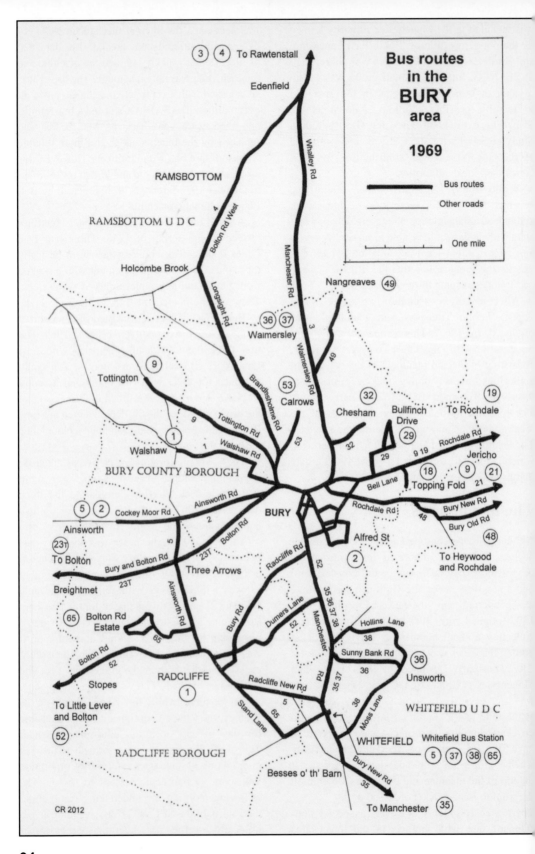

LIFE AFTER BURY

Into SELNEC

Things did not change overnight. The PTE organised the eleven former municipal bus undertakings into three divisions, Northern, Central and Southern, Bury combining with Ramsbottom to become a District of the Northern Division, which had its headquarters in the former Bolton Corporation Transport offices in Bradshawgate. In addition to Bury and Ramsbottom the Northern Division also included Bolton, Rochdale and Leigh. Bury contributed a total of 96 buses to the new organisation consisting of AEC, Bedford, Daimler and Leyland chassis with a mixture of bodies by Alexander, East Lancs, Metro-Cammell, Weymann and Willowbrook.

The first outward sign of things to come was the new Sunglow Orange and White livery which started to appear on the buses in the following March. At the same time SELNEC's new logo, a stylised 'S' together with the divisional name, was applied to all buses, whether repainted or not and, more controversially, the existing municipal coats of arms were removed from the vehicle sides. Bury's buses gained a magenta 'lazy S' with the name 'NORTHERN' in black. The first Bury bus to be painted in the SELNEC livery was number 6089, the first of the 1967 batch of Daimler Fleetline single-deckers.

The next step was to introduce a unified fleet numbering scheme, Northern Division buses being renumbered between 6000-99. Bury's single-deckers were numbered in the 6000 series and its double-deckers in the 6300 series as follows-

81 KEN 381G to 6081
87-88 TEN 887/988 to 6087-6088
89-91 FEN 89-91E to 6089-6091
92-97 KEN 292-297G to 6092-6097
102-116 REN 102-116 to 6302-6316
117-131 TEN 117-131 to 6317-6331
132-137 AEN 832-837C to 6332-6337
138-143 HEN 538-543F to 6338-6343
201-225 GEN 201-225 to 6351-6375
176-177 BEN 176-177 to 6376-6377
178-184 BEN 174-184 to 6378-6384
186 BEN 186 to 6386
187-190 FEN 587-590E to 6387-6390
1-3 KEN 231-233G to 6391-6393

The new numbers were applied haphazardly and in different styles dependent upon what transfers were available at the time, although it all got sorted out eventually with standard black numerals being applied on repainting. One bus from each constituent undertaking was painted in the new livery and exhibited to the press on Manchester's rain-swept training school yard at Ardwick.

Buses which the Corporation had ordered during the last years of the Department's existence were delivered to SELNEC, initially being allocated to their home depot. Seven Fleetlines with East Lancs bodies like numbers 1-3 arrived in 1970. Painted in SELNEC orange but with the interior in Bury green they took the numbers 6344-50. More interesting was the fate which befell Bury's final order for five more Fleetlines. From the beginning, the PTE had made no secret of its intention to develop a standard double-deck bus and to this end some of the inherited orders still outstanding were modified by SELNEC's engineers as prototypes for the new design. Bury's five Fleetlines emerged in 1972 with Northern Counties bodies, numbered EX12-16 in the PTE experimental series. After evaluation at various depots they came home to Bury in 1974 and were renumbered 6395-6399. All outstanding orders were now delivered and there was a pause while various options were considered.

A start was made on withdrawing the oldest buses and by the end of 1971 16 vehicles had gone; the two remaining AEC Regents, all but two of the Weymann-bodied Leyland PD2s and eight of the PD3s. To balance withdrawals and new deliveries and to speed up the conversion to one-person-operation, transfers of buses within and between the divisions were common. The two remaining PD2s, 6380 and 6386, went to Stalybridge and stayed there, still in Bury green, until they were withdrawn in 1972 and two Fleetlines went to Rochdale being replaced by four new Atlanteans ordered by Bolton. Because of a shortage of single-deck buses in Salford, Fleetlines 6092-6097 went to Weaste, Bury getting five virtually new Oldham Atlanteans 5194-5198 and two elderly Rochdale AEC Regents 6221 and 6222 in exchange. Bury also received Manchester Atlanteans and Fleetlines for further OPO conversions.

Meanwhile, behind the scenes a lot of work was being carried out into standardisation of wages, conditions and operating practices, most of which went unnoticed by the general public, although a necessary but unfortunately timed 15% increase in fares did not. More obvious was the comprehensive service numbering scheme. For a time services continued to show the numbers used by their former operators and it was not until 1972 that SELNEC developed a single unified scheme. Renumbering was implemented in stages over several months starting in November 1972 and Bury services were renumbered on 3rd March 1974, mostly into the 468-499 block. But now more important changes were in the pipeline.

Greater Manchester Transport

As a result of the 1973 Local Government Act the SELNEC Passenger Transport Authority was abolished and overall transport strategy came directly under the control of the newly formed Greater Manchester Council from 1st April 1974. The bus and rail operations became the Greater Manchester PTE with a new 'wiggly M' logo and the title 'Greater Manchester Transport.'

During 1978 No 6316 was repainted into Bury livery with its former number 116 to mark the 75th anniversary of the town's first electric tramcar.

Outwardly, however, little changed. The last half-cab double-deckers, 6387-6390 were withdrawn in 1980 and the last former Bury Corporation bus, number 6392, went in 1982. The last of the Bury orders, the much modified Fleetlines 6395/7-9 lasted until 1985.

The new Bury interchange was opened on 17th March 1980. Costing £4.9 million it incorporated the railway line to Manchester which would eventually become Metrolink, the old Bolton Street station being handed over to the East Lancashire Railway. It fronted on to Kay Gardens and at a stroke did away with all the bus stops around the gardens and in the surrounding streets.

Further re-organisation of the management structure in 1981 created four areas, North, South, East and West, Bury becoming part of the new North area along with Rochdale, Queens Road (Manchester) and the two former Salford depots at Frederick Road and Weaste and, together with the other districts, was reduced to depot status, decision-making being concentrated in the new North Area headquarters at Frederick Road.

Work on a new depot for Greater Manchester Transport started in January 1983 on the site of the former north depot on Rochdale Road. The depot, which cost £5 million, stood on a 5.3 acre site and was designed to hold 100 buses. It was officially opened by the Mayor on 22nd August 1985. The south depot was used for a time for storage until it was demolished in May 1987.

Since the break up and subsequent privatisation of Greater Manchester Buses, First Manchester and Rossendale Transport run most of the local services in Bury. A number of small operators can also be seen, but the apple green and cream Corporation buses are now just a memory.

Daimler Fleetline number 96 (KEN 296G) became SELNEC 6096. It spent most of its life with the PTE working from Weaste depot in Salford and is pictured here with its new orange and white livery while working on service 5 between Salford and Peel Green, a route which needed single-deckers because of the low bridge on Barton Lane. *(MMT)*

Two of Bury's Weymann-bodied Leyland PD2s 180 and 186 went to Stalybridge and are pictured above as 6380 and 6386 standing together in Stalybridge depot. *(SGC)*

When SELNEC took over in 1969 one of the first things it did was to incorporate the small Ramsbottom operation into the new Bury district. In order to convert Ramsbottom to OPO a number of Bury Atlanteans moved there, ousting the Ramsbottom PD2s. One such was number 116 (EEN 116), now 6316, which is seen right arriving at Rawtenstall on the former service 4 from Bury. *(RM)*

In the bottom picture time has moved on and Fleetline 6344 (NEN 504J), one of seven buses ordered by Bury and delivered to SELNEC, heads down the interchange on its way to Walmersley, now displaying the Greater Manchester 'Wiggly M' on its side. On the right Bury's SELNEC standard Fleetline number 7172 waits to leave for Bolton. *(SGC)*

APPENDIX 1 - THE TRAM FLEET

Year	Fleet Nos	Builder	Type	Trucks	Notes
1903	1-14	Milnes	Open-top bogie	McGuire No 3 MT	1
1903	15-28	Milnes	Open-top 4-wheel	McGuire Colombian	2 3
1904	29-34	BECC	Balcony 4-wheel	Mountain and Gibson type C	4
1905	35	Wilson and Stockhill	Balcony 4-wheel	Mountain and Gibson type C	
1906	36-41	Brush	Balcony 4-wheel	Mountain and Gibson 21EM	
1907	42-47	UECC	Balcony 4-wheel	Mountain and Gibson 21EM	
1910	48-50	UECC	Balcony 4-wheel	Mountain and Gibson 21EM	
1913	51-54	UECC	Balcony 4-wheel	Mountain and Gibson 21EM	
1925	55-60	English Electric	Enclosed bogie	Burnley MT	5

Notes
1. All rebuilt 1925/6 as totally enclosed with English Electric Burnley-type bogies.
2. All fitted with open-balcony top covers by Wilson and Stockhill or UECC in 1905/6. Cars 15, 21 and two others, which became 30 and 36, rebuilt as totally enclosed in 1926. Car 30 was rebuilt with EMB trucks in 1930 for use on the Heywood-Manchester service.
3. Car 21 became Bolton 331 in 1943.
4. Car 30 became Sunderland 85 in 1947.
5. Cars 55, 56 and 58 became Bolton 451-453 in 1943.

APPENDIX 2 – BUS FLEET LIST

Year	Reg. Nos.	Fleet Nos.	Chassis	Body	Notes
1925	EN 2630-2631	1-2	Leyland C7	Leyland B26F	
1925	EN 2700	3	Leyland C7	Leyland B26F	
1926	EN 2903	4	Leyland A13	Leyland B26F	
1926	EN 3000	5	Leyland A13	Leyland B26F	
1927	EN 3486-3489	6-9	Leyland PLSC3	Leyland B30D	
1927	EN 3525-3526	10-11	Leyland PLSC3	Leyland B30D	
1929	EN 4310-4313	12-15	Leyland LT1	Roe B31D	
1929	EN 4314-4317	16-19	Dennis EV	Roe B30D	
1930	EN 4500-4503	20-23	Leyland TD1	Massey H24/24D	
1930	EN 4721	29	AEC Regal	Brush B30D	
1930	EN 4722	30	Leyland TS3	Vulcan B32D	
1930	EN 4723	31	Crossley Alpha	Vulcan B32D	
1931	BN 4190	24	Leyland A13	?	1
1931	EN 4741-4742	25-26	Leyland TD1	Brush H24/24D	
1931	EN 4743	27	AEC Regent	Brush H24/24D	
1931	EN 4744	28	Crossley Condor	Brush H24/24D	
1931	EN 5010-5014	32-36	Crossley Condor	Crossley H24/24D	
1931	EN 4701	37	Crossley Condor	Crossley L24/24R	
1931	TE 9855	24	Leyland TD1	Leyland H24/24R	2
1932	EN 5290-5294	1-5	Daimler CP6	Strachans H28/20D	
1933	TE 8365	38	Leyland TD1	Leyland L24/24RO	3
1933	EN 5632-5633	39-40	AEC Regent	NCME H26/22D	
1933	EN 5634-5641	41-48	AEC Regent	Roe H26/22D	

1934	EN 5980	49	Crossley Mancunian	EE H26/22C	
1934	EN 5981	50	Leyland TD3c	EE H26/22C	
1935	EN 6050-6054	51-55	Leyland TT2	EE H33/27C	
1936	EN 6712-6718	56-62	Leyland TD4c	Leyland H24/24R	
1937	EN 6971-6974	31/4/5/7	Leyland TD4c	Leyland H24/24R	4
1938	EN 7291-7299	63-71	Leyland TD5c	Leyland H26/26R	5
1938	EN 7701-7704	72/3/5/4	Leyland TS8c	Burlingham B36F	6
1939	EN 8113-8117	76-80	Leyland TD5	NCME H30/26R	
1940	EN 8249-8253	81-85	Leyland TD7	NCME H30/26R	7
1940	EN 8245-8248	86-89	Leyland TD7	Weymann H30/26R	8
1943	EN 8407/8/14	11/28/33	Daimler CWA6	Massey H30/26R	9
1946	EN 8531-8535	97-101	Crossley DD42/3	Crossley H30/26R	
1946	EN 8536-8550	102-116	Leyland PD1	Roe H31/25R	
1946/47	EN 8811-8819	117-125	Leyland PD1	NCME H30/26R	
1947	EN 8820-8823	126-129	Leyland PD1A	NCME H30/26R	
1947	EN 8824-8827	130-133	Leyland PS1	Roe B35R	10
1947	EN 9034-9048	134-148	Leyland PD1A	Weymann H30/26R	
1948	EN 9180-9181	149-150	Guy Wolf	Barnard B20F	
1949	EN 9551-9559	151-159	Leyland PD2/4	Weymann H30/26R	
1950	EN 9960-9975	160-175	Leyland PD2/4	Weymann H30/26R	
1952	BEN 176-177	176-177	AEC Regent III	Weymann H30/26R	
1953	BEN 178-186	178-186	Leyland PD2/3	Weymann H30/26R	
1957	FEN 81-86	81-86	AEC Reliance	Weymann B43F	
1958/59	GEN 201-225	201-225	Leyland PD3/6	Weymann H41/32RD	
1960	LEN 101	101	Gut Wulfrunian	Park Royal H43/30F	
1963	REN 102-116	102-116	Leyland PDR1/1	MCCW H41/33F	
1964	TEN 117-131	117-131	Daimler CRG6LX	Alexander H43/31F	
1964	TEN 887/998	87-88	AEC Reliance	Alexander B43F	
1965	AEN 832-837C	132-137	Daimler CRG6LX	East Lancs H43/31F	
1967	FEN 89-91E	89-91	Daimler SRG6LX	East Lancs B41D	
1967	FEN 587-590E	187-190	Leyland PD2/37	East Lancs H37/25F	
1968	HEN 538-543F	138-143	Daimler CRG6LX	East Lancs H45/31F	
1969	KEN 231-233G	1-3	Leyland PDR1A/1	East Lancs H45/27D	
1969	KEN 381G	81	Bedford J2SZ10	Willowbrook B21F	
1969	KEN 292-297G	92-97	Daimler CRG6LX	East Lancs B41D	
1970	NEN 504-510J		Daimler CRG6LX	East Lancs H45/28D	11

1. Ex W Lees, Radcliffe, new 1921. Operated for about three months in Lees's blue livery.
2. Ex Leyland demonstrator, new 1929.
3. Ex HG Orr, Little Lever, new 1929. Staircase enclosed 1935/36.
4. Renumbered 81-84 1945/46.
5. 70 received a new Northern Counties H30/26R body in 1943.
6. 74/5 exchanged fleet numbers in 1951. All four were converted to TD5s in 1951 and received new Massey H30/56R bodies.
7. Renumbered 6-10 by 1941 and 85-89 1945/6.
8. Renumbered 16-19 by 1941 and 90-93 1945/6.
9. Renumbered 94-96 1945/6.
10. Rebuilt to B35F by Northern Counties in 1954 for OMO.
11. Bury Corporation order intended to be numbered 4-10, but delivered to SELNEC PTE as numbers 6344-6350.

SELNEC SERVICE NUMBERING

Bury Corporation tended to use individual numbers for all short workings and works and schools services. There is no complete record of the dates when most of these started or finished and many just faded away gradually. Those remaining at the implementation of the SELNEC numbering scheme on 3rd March 1974 were absorbed into the main service.

BURY No	Route	SELNEC No
1	Walshaw - Bury – Radcliffe via Warth	481
2	Ainsworth – Bury – Alfred St	472
3	Bury – Rawtenstall – Water	473
4	Bury – Ramsbottom – Rawtenstall	474, 475
5	Whitefield – Radcliffe – Ainsworth	484
9	Jericho – Bury – Tottington	479
12	Bury – Starling (Shorts on 2)	472
14	Bury – Heywood (Shorts on 21)	471
16	Bury – Radcliffe – Stopes (Shorts on 52)	524
18	Bury – Topping Fold	478
19	Bury – Jericho – Rochdale	469
21	Bury – Heywood – Rochdale	471
23T	Bury – Breightmet – Bolton	523
26	Bury – Breightmet (Shorts on 23T)	523
29	Bury – Bullfinch Drive	489
32	Bury – Chesham Road	493
33	Bury – Tottington.(Shorts on 9)	479
35	Bury – Whitefield – Manchester	35
36	Walmersley – Bury – Sunny Bank	486
37	Walmersley – Bury – Whitefield	487
38	Bury – Unsworth – Whitefield	488
41	Bury – Peel Mill (Works service)	906
42	Bury - Heap Bridge (Works service)	907
45	Bury – Old Duke (Shorts on 4)	474
46	Bury - Bradley Fold (Works service)	908
48	Bury – Heywood	468
49	Bury – Nangreaves	499
50	Elton Schools - Old Duke	904
51	Elton Schools - Lichfield Drive	905
52	Bury – Radcliffe – Bolton	524
53	Bury – Calrows	493
56	Bury Grammar School – Walmersley	900
58	Elton Schools - Bury Bridge	898
59	Bury Grammar School - Jericho	899
60	Lichfield Drive - Old Duke (School service)	903
65	Whitefield – Radcliffe – Bolton Road Estate	485

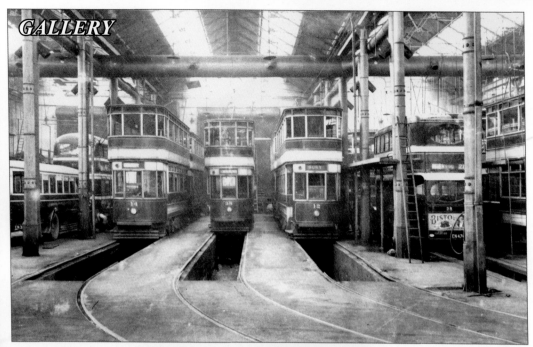

In the photograph above, taken in the depot in April 1937, a mixture of trams and buses stand over the pits. The single-decker on the left is one of six Leyland Lions of 1927 vintage while number 28 on the right is a Brush-bodied Crossley Condor dating from 1931. *(DBC)*

On the left are two photographs of tram number 30, the car which was rebuilt for the Heywood to Manchester route. It is shown in the depot, also in April 1937, and in the lower view is seen after its sale to Sunderland, complete with a pantograph and the mandatory 'Shop at Binns' advert. *(MMT upper, ADP lower)*

After the war only one full tram service remained running between Tottington and Walmersley. In the winter of 1946 hats and overcoats are much in evidence as Saturday shoppers crowd the pavements of The Rock while a tired looking tram number 13 passes by on its way to Walmersley. *(MMT)*

Two years later and looking even more shabby number 13 is pictured again below standing at Walmersley terminus while its crew chat, possibly about the fortunes of the Shakers, Bury's football team. *(ADP)*

Tram number 59 seems to have been very popular with the photographers. It was one of Bury's newest cars dating from 1925 and worked right up until the end of tramway operation. It is pictured above in 1945 leaving the Market Place for Tottington while in the background a Brush-bodied Leyland TD1 turns from The Rock into Market Street on its way in from Jericho on service 9. *(MMT)*

The upper picture on the right shows number 59 again a year later as a long queue of intending passengers board at the Market Place on their way home to Tottington. *(DBC)*

Finally, it is now 1948 and the Tottington line has closed leaving the remaining trams to shuttle between Bury and Walmersley. Number 59 looks even more neglected as it stands in the short spur at the top of Market Street after arriving from Walmersley. *(DBC)*

Buses dominate the photograph of Kay Gardens above taken in the early thirties. On the left a Massey-bodied Leyland Titan TD1, probably number 23 (EN 4503) dating from 1930, is leaving Moss Street on service 2 to Ainsworth while another of the class stands across the Gardens in Haymarket Street. *(DBC)*

The view of the modern sunken workshops below could not have been taken earlier than 1935 as one of the Leyland Titanics stands in the centre of the row of buses over the pits. *(SGC)*

In the picture above number 52 (EN 605), one of the six Titanics which were purchased in 1935 to replace the trams on the Jericho route, turns left from The Rock into Market Street on its inward journey to Bury. *(DBC)*

The same bus is shown below working in the opposite direction as it stands in The Rock, demonstrating its ability to clear queues as passengers board for Jericho through the centre entrance. *(SGC)*

In June 1936 Bury took delivery of seven Leyland Titan double-deckers with Leyland 54-seat bodies, although a further row of four seats was quickly added to the upper deck. These were the TD4c model fitted with torque converters and were ordered to cater for service enhancements. Number 57 (EN 6713) is seen in the picture above circling the roundabout in Rochdale town centre while working the former express service 23 between there and Bolton. It was the first of the batch to be withdrawn in December 1947 and saw further service in Northern Ireland. *(DBC)*

Below number 58 (EN 6714) stands at the head of a line of buses in Market Street while working on the Ainsworth service. It was withdrawn in 1948 and scrapped. *(SGC)*

Examples of Bury's last pre-war orders are pictured here. Number 72 (EN 7701) shown was unusual in that it was originally a Leyland Tiger TS8c single-decker but was rebuilt in 1951 as a TD5 and received a new Massey double-deck body. It is shown above in this form parked on Knowsley Street after the morning peak. It was withdrawn in 1958 and passed to Paton Brothers of Renfrew. *(SGC)*

On the right, number 76 (EN 8113) was the first of five Leyland TD5s with Northern Counties bodies delivered in August 1939. It is seen right parked between peaks on Market Street next to the fairground. *(RM)*

Number 86 (EN 8245), a Weymann-bodied Leyland TD7, was not delivered until 1940. It was renumbered to 16 by 1941 and again to 90 in 1946, the number it is carrying in the lower picture, standing in Knowsley Street. Moss Street and Kay Gardens can be seen in the left background. *(SGC)*

Pictured top left in Haymarket Street on its way to Walshaw on service 1, number 111 (EN 8545), a Roe-bodied Leyland PD1 delivered in 1946, stands alongside a Morris Commercial van. It was withdrawn in 1959 and exported to Split in Yugoslavia. *(SGC)*

In the centre, number 129 (EN 8823), a Leyland PD1A with Northern Counties body, stands on The Mosses, an area of open ground off Market Street to the south of Kay Gardens which was used as a parking ground until it was submerged under the new Angouleme Way in the early eighties. *(DBC)*

Below: Passengers study the timetable on the bus stop as number 120 (EN 8814), a similar PD1 model, waits in Haymarket Street for a relief crew to take it on to Radcliffe. *(DBC)*

Three views of the 1947 Roe-bodied Leyland Tiger PS1 single-deckers. There were four of these rugged buses, initially with a rear entrance for crew operation on the services to Ramsbottom, Edenfield and Rawtenstall. Later they were rebuilt with a front entrance for one-person-operation of the Heywood local service until ousted by the AEC Reliances when they moved to other more lightly used routes.

In the two pictures on the right number 131 (EN 8825) is pictured in Moss Street outside the Art Gallery *(ADJ)* and parked on The Mosses. *(SGC)* It was withdrawn in 1963 and passed to local builder Milligan, Rooney and Quinn for employees' transport.

Below, number 133 (EN 8827) stands in Moss Street next to the Market. The ornate building in the background is the former Market Hall on the corner of Market Street which disappeared in the wholesale redevelopment of the seventies. Withdrawn in 1962, it saw further service in Scotland with Bennett of Kilsyth. *(DBC)*

From 1947 to 1959 Bury standardised on Weymann bodies for its double-deckers, six of which are shown on these pages. In the picture above, 1947 Leyland Titan PD1A number 143 (EN 9043) stands outside the Ramsbottom Corporation depot in Stubbins Lane while working on service 4 between Rawtenstall and Bury on which double-deckers had replaced single-deckers in 1954. *(STA)*

On the left, Leyland Titan PD2/4 number 152 (EN 9552) dating from 1949 has just turned round at the Old Duke on Brandlesholme Road ready to work back to Bury on a very wet morning. *(SGC)*

In the lower picture, on a much better day number 158 of the same batch is seen standing in Moss Street before leaving on service 29 to Bullfinch Drive, or the Dicky Bird estate as it was more commonly known. A typical conductor of the time with his summer jacket rolled up at the sleeves, his cash bag and ticket machine box is chatting to a trendy young lady pushing a fashionable buggy. *(MMT)*

Of the 76 double-deckers delivered in this period all but two were on Leyland chassis. The odd ones were a pair of AEC Regent IIIs delivered in October 1952, one of which, number 177,(BEN 177) is pictured parked on The Mosses next to Leyland Titan PD2/4 number 171. Both buses passed to SELNEC and were withdrawn in 1971. Number 177 is now preserved at the Greater Manchester Museum of Transport. *(SGC)*

Number 178 (BEN 178) was a Leyland Titan PD2/3, the first of nine which arrived in the summer of 1953. It is pictured on the right parked in Market Street while passengers wait at the shelter for a bus to Bolton. *(AM)*

Number 186 (BEN 186), the last PD2 to be delivered to Bury in July 1953, is seen on Walmersley Road on its way into Bury from Water and Rawtenstall on service 3. It became SELNEC 6386 in 1969 and was withdrawn and scrapped four years later. *(SGC)*

Bury's first buses of the modern era to be designed specifically for one-person-operation were six AEC Reliances with Weymann 43-seat front-entrance bodies. They arrived in 1957 and were used to convert services 20 (Whitefield-Radcliffe-Ainsworth) and 38 (Bury-Whitefield via Unsworth). Number 85 (FEN 85) stands (above) in Knowsley Street with one of the iconic PD3 Titans behind. Arguably Bury's best known buses, these 25 vehicles, new in 1958, gave sterling service over the years. Number 213 (GEN 213) is seen below climbing up Burnley Road East out of Waterfoot on its way from Bury to Water on service 3. *(Both SGC)*

Apart from the OPO routes the PD3s could be seen everywhere across the system as well as in the neighbouring towns. Number 216 (GEN 216) is seen above arriving at Walshaw, the terminus of Bury's original bus route which retained the number 1 until the SELNEC renumbering of 1973/4. *(SGC)*

Rain and slippery cobbles make for tricky driving conditions as another PD3 turns right out of Knowsley Street into Moss Street, watched by a couple of pedestrians waiting to cross. *(STA)*

Below, Doug Jack manages to catch another wet day in Bury as number 221 (GEN 221) stands in Haymarket Street while working on service 37 from Walmersley to Whitefield. *(ADJ)* Both these buses ran in service for 17 years before being withdrawn and scrapped in 1975.

The story of Lenny, the ill-fated Guy Wulfrunian number 101 (LEN 101) has been told in detail earlier. There is little doubt that it was the most widely discussed and most photographed of all Bury's buses during its short life with the Corporation, so it seems appropriate that it should be featured prominently in this section.

In the picture on the left it is seen in the depot when new displaying the route number 9, on which it would spend much of its time when actually running in service. Below, it is viewed from the rear standing in Broad Street before leaving for Jericho. The Rochdale bus in front is one the last batch of AEC Regent Vs fitted with platform doors which is waiting to leave for home on service 19. *(DBC upper, SGC lower)*

On the opposite page a forlorn Lenny stands in the depot after being taken out of service in October 1963, the indicator blinds already removed for use elsewhere.

The final picture, taken while under restoration, gives a good idea of the cramped cab and hot and noisy conditions the driver would have endured with the forward engine taking up much of the space. *(Both DBC)*

Top: The first of the 1963 batch of Metro-Cammell-bodied Leyland Atlanteans, number 102 (REN 102), leaves Radcliffe and heads for Bury on service 52. Behind can just be seen a Salford Daimler working on the long peripheral service 6 to Swinton and Eccles. Number 102 became SELNEC 6302 and after withdrawal in 1977 passed to NV-Imnoly of Landogen in Belgium. *(MMT)*

Below: Another of the same batch of Atlanteans, number 111 (REN 111) was working on service 16 between Bury and Stopes, a short on service 52, when it was photographed standing in Haymarket Street. *(SGC)*

Top: Alexander-bodied Daimler Fleetline number 131 (TEN 131) was the last of 25 such buses which went into service in 1964. It is pictured in one of the photographers' favourite locations, Moss Street on the south side of Kay Gardens, while working on service 37 between Whitefield and Walmersley. *(SGC)*

Below Number 120 (TEN 120), another of the same batch is pictured climbing up out of Heywood towards Summit while heading for home from Rochdale on service 21. Apart from the learner in the Ford Prefect there would appear to be no traffic on what was the A58 trunk road. *(MMT)*

Above: Alexander-bodied Daimler Fleetline number 123 (TEN 123) is photographed passing Ryecroft Farm between Rochdale and Heywood on service 21. It became SELNEC 6323 and was one of the first of its batch to be withdrawn in 1976. *(SGC)*

Below: Two AEC Reliances, also with Alexander bodies, were delivered at the same time for use on one-person operated services. Number 88 (TEN 988) is pictured in the depot when new. *(SGC)*

Above: Number 137 (AEN 837C) was a Daimler Fleetline with a 74-seat East Lancs body which arrived in 1965. Now SELNECs 6337 it is shown being photographed standing in Haymarket Street while working on service 21 to Rochdale. *(DBC)*

Below: Another East Lancs-bodied Fleetline number 6335 (AEN 835C), formerly Bury 135, heads for Whitefield on service 37. It was withdrawn in 1978 and ended its days in Sussex with Fisher and Redford of Chichester. *(SGC)*

Bury's last deliveries of full-size buses before the SELNEC takeover also carried East Lancs bodies. They were designed for one-person-operation and were painted in a new modern livery with more cream and less green. In the upper picture single-deck Fleetline number 94 (KEN 294G) stands in Knowsley Street *(MMT)* while below a queue of passengers boards Leyland Atlantean number 2 (KEN 232G) in Moss Street on service 29 to Bullfinch Drive, the first route to be operated by OPO double-deckers. *(DBC)*

There was a time when, instead of buying new, service vehicles were cut down from withdrawn buses. The vehicle above was originally Number 21 (EN 4501), a Leyland Titan TD1 with Massey double-deck body dating from 1930. Withdrawn in 1946 it became Bury's towing wagon number 202. In 1955 it was sold to the Light Railway League and later passed to the Tramway Museum Society. *(MMT)*

Number 64 (EN 7292) was a Leyland TD5c with Leyland double-deck body new in 1938. It was withdrawn in 1951 and became towing vehicle number 204, later being renumbered 24 as in the upper picture on the right.

Guy Wolf number 149 (EN 9180), on the lower right, was one of a pair of small buses bought in 1948 to work the Nangreaves service. It was withdrawn in 1954 and cut down to a lorry for the maintenance gang, originally numbered 202 and later 22 before being withdrawn in 1961 and sold to become a breakdown crane. *(Both DBC)*

Upper left: Bury ran joint with Bolton on two routes between the towns, 23 via Breightmet and 52 via Radcliffe and Little Lever. Leyland PD1A number 127 (EN 8821) is seen braving the Bolton weather as it runs along a very wet Moor Lane on service 23. Officially the service was numbered 23T (for tram) to distinguish it from the former Bolton-Bury-Rochdale express service withdrawn in 1939. Bury showed either but Bolton always showed the T, using 23 for the Breightmet shorts. *(DBC)*

Lower left: Number 221 (GEN 221) stands in Moor Lane on service 52 next to a Bolton PD2 on its way to Dunscar. *(SGC)*

Below: On another wet Bolton day number 189 (FEN 589E) leaves the stop on Bradshawgate and pulls out to pass a Bolton PD2 on its way to Crossdale Road. *(DBC)*

Above: Bury also ran into Rochdale on two routes, 19 via Jericho and 21 via Heywood. Again, there was confusion with service numbers, the official version being 21T (This time for Tweedale Street). Bury usually used the T but Rochdale showed 21, reserving 21T for Heywood shorts. Bury Leyland PD1 number 123 (EN 8817) stands in Rochdale's South Parade, alongside a pair of Rochdale buses. *(DBC)*

Below: Service 35 to Manchester was jointly operated with Manchester and Salford Corporations. Here, one of Salford's ubiquitous Daimlers runs along Market Street on its way to Manchester with the ornate Market Hall in the background. *(MMT)*

Inside and out. Two views of single-deck Daimler Fleetline number 91 (FEN 91E), standing on Knowsley Street (top) and an interior view (below). *(Both DBC)*

In July 1967 20 members of the Bury Chess Club left the town on a trip to Poland on recently withdrawn Leyland PD2/4 number 151 (EN 9551) which they had purchased for the sum of £106. The first part of the journey through England was uneventful, but once across the Channel the party realised that clearances across the Continent were not enough for an English double-decker bus. Eventually, even with a police escort to avoid low bridges it became apparent that number 151 was not going to get to Poland in its present form, so the decision was made to take the top off and this done, the party completed the tour and arrived back in Bury to schedule.

Number 151 is pictured above in Germany in its original form and on the right after arriving back in Bury as modified. *(Both DBC)*

Above: Many of Bury's buses were in good condition when withdrawn and were consequently in demand for further service with small independent operators. Several travelled north of the border and number 72 (EN 7701), one of the former Leyland Tiger single-deckers rebodied by Massey in 1951, went to Paton of Renfrew who took a large number of second hand English buses. *(DBC)*

Below: In 1964 Paton took five Weymann-bodied Leyland PD2/4s dating from 1950. Number 161 (EN 9961), now number 84 in Paton's fleet, is pictured working between Govan and Paisley. *(DBC)*

Above: Two more former Bury buses of the same batch, numbers 171 (EN 9971) and 175 (EN 9975) stand at Renfrew Ferry waiting for custom. They were withdrawn in 1967. *(DBC)*

Below: Number 166 (EN 9966) also went to Scotland but led a somewhat different life as a driver training vehicle for the General School of Motoring in Glasgow. *(SGC)*

Above: Number 11, later 94 (EN 8407), a wartime Daimler CWA6 fitted with a new Roe body in 1952, went to Armstrong of Westerhope in Newcastle-upon-Tyne where it is pictured in the depot yard. *(DBC)*

Below: Weymann-bodied Leyland TD7 number 87 (EN 8246) was withdrawn in 1952 and sold to Lansdowne Luxury Coaches Ltd of Leytonstone in east London. It is pictured here, repainted into Birmingham style livery. *(DBC)*

Above: By contrast, Leyland Tiger PS1 number 132 (EN 8826) remained in Bury and was one of a pair (the other was number 130) that was purchased by Milligan, Rooney and Quinn Ltd (MRQ Construction) for use as a staff bus. *(DBC)*

Below: Finally Leyland PD3 number 203 (GEN 203) was withdrawn in 1971 and passed to Voy of Central Garage, Newton Aycliffe in County Durham. *(DBC)*

THEN AND NOW

Just over a hundred years separates this pair of photographs of Rochdale Old Road at Fairfield but there is remarkably little change in the intervening period. In the upper picture taken in 1910 a tram climbs up to the terminus at the distinctive George and Dragon pub opposite the entrance to the workhouse. *(SGC)* Below in June 2012 the stone setts have been covered in tarmac and there is more traffic as a Rossendale Transport Volvo turns right into what is now the access road to Fairfield Hospital. *(CR)*

Although much has changed in Bolton Street in the intervening 75 years, one building that has survived virtually unchanged and even for the same use is the Billiard Hall. In 1937, tram number 56 climbs up from Bury Bridge on its way from Tottington to Walmersley. While much of the street has been redeveloped the old hall remains, and is now the Bury Snooker Club. In June 2012 a Rossendale Transport Plaxton-bodied Dennis Dart is pictured at the same spot on its way into town from Holcombe Brook on service 481. *(MMT upper, CR lower)*

Number 121 (EN 8815) was a Northern Counties-bodied Leyland PD1 new in 1947. It is pictured above standing in Moss Street in the early fifties before leaving for Tottington on service 33. *(DBC)* In the lower picture taken some 60 years later the Knowsley Hotel and the other buildings on Haymarket Street are little changed, but Moss Street has now been submerged under the interchange where one of First Manchester's articulated Volvos is loading for Manchester on service 135. *(CR)*

In the summer of 1967 a sparkling new number 189 (FEN 589E) swings from Market Street into Haymarket Street on the final few yards of its journey from Bolton, followed by an Alexander-bodied Fleetline *(SGC)*, while below a First Manchester Mercedes-Benz Citaro makes the same manoeuvre some 45 years later. While the Athenaeum building can still be seen on the far left the remainder of Market Street in now pedestrianised and the Millgate shopping centre has been built across the upper part of Haymarket Street. *(CR)*

A quartet of Weymann-bodied Leyland Titans. Number 165 (EN 9965), a PD2/4 model from 1950, stands in Moss Street on the south side of Kay Gardens, above, with a good load of passengers bound for Whitefield, while in the background a Salford Daimler turns out of Haymarket Street en-route for Manchester. Number 165 was withdrawn in 1965 but remained with the Transport Department as a breakdown crane. *(MMT)*

In the centre another PD2/4, number 172 (EN 9972), drops passengers off along Bolton Road on its way to Bolton. *(DBC)*

Two of Bury's PD2/3s dating from 1953 survived into SELNEC, moving to the ex-SHMD depot at Stalybridge. Numbers 180 (BEN 180) and 186 (BEN 186) were renumbered 6380 and 6386 and were both withdrawn in 1973. The former is seen in Hyde bus station with a selection of former SHMD buses and a solitary NWRC vehicle in 1972. *(JAS)*

Bury's first buses designed for OPO were six Weymann-bodied AEC Reliances delivered in 1957. Number 86 (FEN 86) is pictured right standing on Knowsley Street having worked in from Nangreaves. It was withdrawn in 1969. *(MMT)*

Number 88 (TEN 988) was one of a pair of Alexander-bodied AEC Reliances which were new in 1964. It became SELNEC number 6088 in 1969 and was withdrawn in 1977. It is seen on the right on a winter's day dropping down from Nangreaves on a service 49 journey. *(DBC)*

Below is the little-loved Lenny, Guy Wulfrunian number 101 (LEN 101) which arrived in Bury in 1960 to a fanfare of publicity and left much more quietly three years later. It spent much of its time off the road and when working was generally to be found on service 9 where it is pictured at Tottington terminus. It is now in the hands of the Greater Manchester Museum of Transport. *(DBC)*

The 25 Leyland PD3s were arguably Bury's best known vehicles with their smart but functional lines. All passed to SELNEC and some went on to work for Scottish operators. In the upper picture number 204 (GEN 204) stands in Rawtenstall on its way to Bury with a trio of Rawtenstall buses in the background. Below number 214 (GEN 214), now SELNEC number 6364, stands at the Walshaw terminus of service 1. *(Both DBC)*

On a summer evening number 224 (GEN 224), now SELNEC 6374, passes Bolton Street station on its way to Bolton on service 23. *(SGC)* In the picture below, number 224 pauses in Haymarket Street while working cross-town from Walmersley to Whitefield on service 37. A Bolton PD2 adds colour to the scene as it arrives in Bury on service 23T. *(DBC)*

After the experience with the Guy Wulfrunian Bury's next order delivered in April 1963 was for 15 conventional Leyland Atlanteans with a rugged no frills body by Metro-Cammell, the only concession to fashion being the peak over the front of the upper deck. Number 110 (REN 110), pictured above in Haymarket Street, became SELNEC 6310 and ran for 16 years before being withdrawn in 1979. *(DBC)*

On the left another of the class, number 115 (REN 115), is seen after a summer cloudburst further along Haymarket Street on its way to Bolton passing a Rochdale Fleetline about to leave for its home town. *(DBC)*

In the lower picture number 127 (TEN 127), one of the 1964 order for 15 Alexander-bodied Fleetlines, stands in Rochdale town centre as passengers board for the return journey to Bury. *(MMT)*

Market day in Bury. In the upper picture East Lancashire-bodied Daimler Fleetline number 134 (AEN 834C), dating from 1965, shares a crowded Moss Street with market traffic before leaving for Walmersley. It would become SELNEC 6334 but stayed in Bury until it was withdrawn in 1978. In the background the Art Cinema across Knowsley Street and the Art Gallery further down Moss Street still remain but the bus stand is now part of the interchange and the market has moved. In the lower view 1968 Fleetline number 141 (HEN 541F) with East Lancashire body is seen on its way to Bolton via Radcliffe and Little Lever. It became SELNEC 6341 and was withdrawn in 1981. *(Both DBC)*

In 1967 Bury purchased four Leyland Titan PD2/37s with East Lancashire front-entrance bodies for service 23T to Bolton, passing over Trinity Street Station bridge which had a weight restriction precluding the use of heavier buses on the route.

In the upper view number 187 (FEN 587E) turns out of Market Street into Haymarket Street on its way to Bolton. *(MMT)* It became SELNEC 6387 and was withdrawn in 1980, passing to Silver Fox of Glasgow before moving to United Automobile as a training vehicle, in which role it is seen on the left. *(DBC)*

In the lower picture number 188 (FEN 588E) stands in Market Street at one of the wrought iron shelters that were erected with much publicity in the 1930s. This part of Market Street is now pedestrianised and the interchange and the internal by-pass have cut the street in two. *(SGC)*

Number 93 (KEN 293G) was one of four Daimler Fleetlines with single deck bodies by East Lancashire Coach builders which carried the revised livery with more cream applied to the 1969 deliveries. It is pictured outside the depot when new accompanied by one of the 1963 Atlanteans. *(SGC)* Below is number 81 (KEN 381G), the last bus delivered to the Corporation in July 1969, a Bedford J2 with Willowbrook body ordered for the Chesham Road service. It became SELNEC 6081 and worked much of its life in Ramsbottom before withdrawal in 1976. *(MMT)*

The last double-deckers delivered to Bury in 1969 were three Leyland Atlanteans with East Lancs two-door bodies specifically designed for one-person-operation. They arrived in the new mostly cream livery and were numbered 1-3 (KEN 231-3G). They were given SELNEC fleet numbers 6391-3 and as such are seen (top) lined up on the depot yard. *(DBC)* A further seven Daimler Fleetlines with similar bodies, intended to be numbers 4-10 were delivered to SELNEC in orange livery as its 6344-50 the following year. Number 6349 (NEN 509J) is pictured travelling along Haymarket Street on its way to Whitefield. *(MMT)*

Preserved Leyland Titan PD3/6 number 201 (GEN 201), the first of its batch, is owned by Miss Janet Broadhead and can often be seen at Museum events and is pictured above in immaculate condition. *(MMT)* In the lower picture it is parked outside the Greater Manchester Museum of Transport in Boyle Street, flanked by other preserved former Bury buses, Leyland Atlantean 113 (REN 113) and AEC Regent III 177 (BEN 177). *(SGC)*

The only remaining trace of Bury Corporation's once proud Transport Department, which had provided tram and bus services in the Borough and surrounding districts for 66 years, is the former town centre offices in the Market Place which is now a wine bar. *(CR)*